GRACE AND POISON

Grace & POISON

The Small Words in My Body
and *The Disorder of Love*
in one volume

KAREN CONNELLY

TURNSTONE PRESS

The Small Words in My Body was originally published
by Kalamalka Press in 1990.
The Disorder of Love was originally published
by Gutter Press in 1997.

Turnstone Press
607–100 Arthur Street
Artspace Building
Winnipeg, Manitoba
R3B 1H3 Canada
www.TurnstonePress.com

Turnstone Press gratefully acknowledges the assistance of
The Canada Council for the Arts, the Manitoba Arts Council
and the Book Publishing Industry Development Program,
Government of Canada, for our publishing activities.

The Canada Council | Le Conseil des Arts
for the Arts | du Canada

Canadä

Original cover photograph by Hélène Cyr
Design by Manuela Dias

This book was printed and bound in Canada
by Westcan Printing Group for Turnstone Press.

Canadian Cataloguing in Publication Data

Connelly, Karen, 1969–
Grace and poison

Poems.
ISBN 0-88801-264-0

I. Title. II. Title: Small words in my body. III. Title:
Disorder of love
PS8555.O546G7 2001   C811'.54   C2001-910817-6
PR9199.3.C6376G7 2001

For Jackie Henry, my remarkable mother.

For Nancy Holmes and Alexandra Keim,
friends of my heart.

For Libby Oughton,
me agapi yia to spitaki, ta dendra, kai ola ta ala.

ACKNOWLEDGEMENTS

I would like to acknowledge the literary journals and magazines where some of these poems first appeared: *Arc, The Antigonish Review, blue buffalo, Canadian Woman's Studies, Descant, Dandelion, Event, Exile, Fiddlehead, Grain, Island* (Australia), *The New Quarterly, Poetry Canada, Pottersfield Portfolio, The Prairie Journal of Canadian Literature, Room of One's Own, Stand* (England).

I thank my editor Nancy Holmes, for her engagement with all these poems and for her friendship. Thanks is also due to many editors and critics who have helped me polish and think about my work, including John Lent, Caroline Lonsdale, and my friend and mentor Libby Oughton. I thank Jackie Henry, as ever and always, for being my mother.

Friends in Greece who inhabit the second half of this work have my deepest gratitude: Yiorgos, Antigone, Amalia, Mireille, Voula, Andreas, and the children. *Yia hara.*

Contents

The best way to know life
is to love many things.

—Vincent Van Gogh

INTRODUCTION

WHEN I WAS FIFTEEN, I LEFT HOME to escape the various disasters and addictions of my family. *The Small Words in My Body* is one history (there are others) of how I negotiated that flight; it is also the start of a long account detailing the costs incurred, the gifts received and lost, through departure. It can be perilous to speak of poetry in general, even of my own poetry, as autobiography, but *The Small Words* is very autobiographical in ways both obvious and deceptive. Every poem in the collection was written before I was twenty, and much of the first half of the book was written when I was fifteen, sixteen, and seventeen. I wrote then, as I write now, to understand the world I live in. If we are fortunate, that world grows, both widening and deepening as we ourselves mature; the first world allotted to us for understanding—and the one that never leaves us—is that of the family.

How odd, how unsurprising. When I was thirty, back to live in Canada for the first time in several years, I reread *Small Words* and it produced little reaction in me: a blank of emotion paired with cool recognition. It had been out of print for a while; I made half-hearted attempts to get it republished. The book was first brought into the world in 1990 by Kalamalka Press, a collective in B.C dedicated to showcasing the work of new writers. They were too small to afford a reprint when the books ran out, so for a long time I sold photocopied versions, then I stopped doing even that.

A new edition was released in 1995 by Gutter Press. The wonderful and maddening Sam Hiyate was also to publish the first edition of *The Disorder of Love*, in 1997, but when the books sold out, Sam didn't have the resources to reprint. *The Disorder of Love* had been published while I was abroad. By the time I returned to Canada, it was also out of print. It was already a ghost-book for me, a communication whose entry into the world seemed to pass unnoticed.

Just a couple of months ago, I approached *The Small Words* again after returning from another sojourn in Thailand, a place that had provided me, in the mid-eighties, with my first experience of healthy family and community life just as my own unhappy childhood was ending. For this reason and for many others, that part of Southeast Asia continues to exert a profound influence on me. Coming to the poems again recently, after Asia, they suddenly felt real again, taut with the pain of my growing up, with the confusion and sorrow I felt when my older sister killed herself, with the images of violence and amputation that haunted my first serious relationship, with the sometimes-hesitant, sometimes unabashed wonder I first experienced in rural Thailand when I went to live there, at seventeen, as an exchange student.

I recognized my vocation from the time I was very young, and though I became quite disciplined in my teens, I did not yet "know" how to write: I was simply writing, sometimes feverishly, sometimes coldly, in a hard tone that was not my own daily voice, but one used to protect myself. That is one of the redeeming features of a writer's life. We can be tougher, and perhaps wiser, on the page than we are during our days. For me, writing had always been connected to power and delight, a sense of self and beyond-self. To name life is to belong to it, even if one feels—as I often did when I was very young—to be locked away from it. Anyone raised under the heavy tarp of a fundamentalist religion will be able to recognize that sense of deep disconnection from the wider world. Even the sturdiest child cannot go unscathed if she has read, and wholeheartedly believes in, the grisly prophecies of the Revelations. Thank (the revised and expanded version of) God that I was so sturdy. It also helped to become dedicated to something other than drugs and alcohol, which was the fate of several family members.

That I had a gift for writing was an act of grace. Knowing this, I took it very seriously. The poems in *The Small Words* were revised, critiqued by other writers, re-revised. Still, I was learning to write, breathing the pure, sharp, rarefied air of the very young writer, and when I wrote it was sometimes out of instinct and sometimes out of desperate groping in the dark. Passionately believing in the power of words to set things right, I was nevertheless suspicious of everyday, "realistic" speech, particularly the dialect I was learning in school, with its dull and stultifying obligations.

One of the poems in the collection, "Languages I Have Failed To Learn," reveals that growing suspicion, and the terrible frustration I experienced as a student. Though I had several extraordinary teachers whom I continue to think of with gratitude, I had some real duds, too. The principal at the high school I attended in Calgary was a frightening man; after his first speech to the brand-new students in the school, I went to the library and looked up the word *fascist* in an etymological dictionary. At fifteen, I knew enough to take the edge off wanting to be a writer by saying *journalist*, but even on hearing that proposed profession, my guidance counsellor suggested I take a short-hand course: then I could always fall back on secretarial work.

Yes, organized education was like having bricks laid in my cranium. The Languages poem was written after a series of incidents in a biology course. When I refused to dissect small mammals, out of a sense of repulsion and violation—I was a rather small mammal myself—my teacher called me an anti-intellectual in front of the rest of the class.

It was a definitive moment for me, when a fissure opened between myself and world as it was constructed. With religion, some sort of split had come years before, but now I understood it in a fully conscious, perhaps adult way. And this time, I chose it. I remember thinking, "Fine. Because I refuse to take part in your desecration, I am an anti-intellectual. I am a writer and an anti-intellectual, which is absurd." But I accepted that more readily than I could accept what the teacher was asking of me; better the absurdity of my own truth than utter senselessness, the mindless jokes of other students over small dead animals, the accumulation of knowledge we would forget, the bags and bags of wet mice, all in the name of this subject called "science."

My father was a big-game hunter, and though my brothers and sisters and I could understand the apparent necessities of hunting—we ate the animals he killed—we each developed intense empathy for animals. I grew up loving and taking care of small creatures: ants, frogs, tiger salamanders, mice, lizards, rabbits. It seemed to me that science, with its extravagant excesses in vivisection, was far worse than hunting. (In my teens, the hunting, too, became untenable, as did the thought of slaughterhouses; I became a vegetarian.) I knew what I knew, and I could not be argued, scolded, or shamed out of my convictions. The small lives were valuable even if they could not speak our language. By extension, the small words, too, were valuable, even if we could not understand them.

There began, I think, a fascination with other modes of knowing, which served as doors out of what I already knew about the world. Knowledge is a door that opens and closes; it is only a passageway, even when we first conceive of it as an escape. Like knowledge, writing (and reading) is both a path in and a path out, letting us move beyond our accustomed borders but also bringing us back, close to home, to the source. Because the great work of poetry is to close distance, to lay bare the unity of disparate things, people, and places, it can transport us to a different realm and bring us to the source simultaneously. I suspect the work of poetry is like the very small child's first experiences in language: given to us by others, these strange sounds come out of our bodies and correspond—mysteriously, arbitrarily, magically—to the surrounding world, even to the world we have not seen.

Though the first poetry I read was in English—the Bible is also a collection of extraordinary poems—reading it was like entering a new language. When I started to live abroad, the surprise and delight of learning other languages echoed the experience of coming to poetry as a child. Quite naturally, I got hooked. Learning a new language is a rebirth, not only of the stumbling speaker but of the whole universe: every single object and idea is born anew. Like a baby, the impulse in this new world is to put everything into your mouth, experiencing it through the skin. As I grew into adulthood, living first in Thailand, then in Spain, and France, and Greece, then again in Southeast Asia, the languages I learned, imperfectly but nevertheless, provided a physical way of understanding the countries and the people among whom I lived.

Ironically, it is hard to describe how immersion in another language provides such deep entrance into a new culture. Though the foreigner remains foreign always, unable to claim ownership to the mythical key that opens another country, sometimes the other country possesses the mythical key that opens the foreigner. Immersion in the language of the place makes this weird and fascinating opening more likely. When one begins to speak and dream in another language, one begins to think about the world, and one's life, in new ways. Different languages are laced, imbued, with diverse approaches to being human.

Once we begin to dig around in the words we use, the invisible connections between language, history, and landscape become overwhelmingly apparent. David Harmon of TerraLingua, an organization dedicated to preserving linguistic diversity (www.terralingua.org), has discovered a clear link between high language diversity and high biodiversity in different parts of the world. Wherever there are many butterflies, big cats, flowering plants, amphibians, and old trees, there are also many languages. But languages are dying even faster than the landscapes to which they are intimately bound: fifty percent of the world's 7,000 languages will probably be dead within a hundred years. Just as deforestation and desert-encroachment destroy ancient ecosystems, the languages and the people that name, protect, and remember those places disappear. When a language dies, the accumulated knowledge that lives inside words also perishes. We become less able to take care of our environment—and it becomes less able to take care of us—when our tongues are severed from it.

* * *

Yes, even the smallest words:

> those curled pink under mossy wood,
> those nestled in branches,
> receive the words,
> > the ones folded silver and cool
> > > in the blades of rain,
> believe those words.

Written in northern Spain, where I lived at nineteen and twenty, the last poem in *The Small Words in My Body* is an almost religious celebration of "the words.'"After the darkness in the first half of the collection, the Thai poems and the passionate song at the book's end bespeak transformation, all the possibilities presented by a new country and a new language when one is young and conscious of choosing one's own life.

"She Arrives in a Loose Blue Skirt" is about the coming of spring, a woman who smells and tastes and sings and moves like Spain in the months of April and May. Her arrival also brings a language that is universal, healing, and, most crucial, comprehensible through the body. In this long celebratory poem, the skin, like everything in the natural world, is pure continuum, tongue and ear and brain and spirit, able to speak and understand all the words. The poem's last image is of a Gypsy woman dancing alone on the beach, catching the rain, "all the words," in her dirty hands and tangled hair. Old, solitary, dirty, illiterate, she is nevertheless chosen to welcome beautiful spring because, like a child or an animal, she still knows how to absorb the world (the words) through her skin.

I am beginning to know her well, and love her better, this beautiful, ugly, passionate, gentle, dangerous solitary woman. Though she has visited me for a long time in different forms, I used to be rather afraid of her. In *The*

Disorder of Love, she is the incomparable (and very real) Voula, a fabulous, tough, and much-maligned woman who lived through several seasons near the Greek village that is my other home. In *This Brighter Prison* (and in a short story in *One Room in a Castle*) the lone woman is Isadora, whom I met on my first trip to Greece in 1989; she is Amaya, too, a heroin addict I knew in Bilbao. In a book I have yet to write, she is also one of the many famed women healers of the Spanish Basque country who fled into the hills near San Sebastian to escape the misogynist violence of the Inquisition.

There is much to be said about the woman alone, defining herself outside and beyond the realm of conventional sexual relationships and children, but that is another essay, or perhaps a long conversation, clamouring with many different voices and stories. It's interesting to note that when many people read the phrase "a woman alone," their first reaction is close to pity: this must be a woman disappointed in love or perhaps unable to bear children. To think of a woman alone is still to think, essentially, and very boringly, of a woman without a man: a deficient female. Suffice it to say that women alone in many different places are some of my most important, most joyful, and most generous teachers and friends, consistently able to reinvent themselves and reimagine the world. They are rarely alone in any terrible or tragic sense—unless not having a man permanently installed in one's home is a viable definition of tragedy. On the contrary, these women's lives are filled with varied and rich friendships, loves, and satisfying work.

The woman alone is persistent; she will not go away. In *The Border Surrounds Us*, published in 2000, she is the voice in "The Old Woman Speaks." Later in the book, solitude itself is personified as a feisty woman tramp, an echo of the frayed, stray Gypsy in *The Small Words*. In the title poem, the poet becomes the lone woman. I face a stone wall and tear it down—a fabulous thing to do, which I recommend to anyone in need of cheap therapy who's not too worried about scorpions—then I "begin, with calloused faith, to dig in the hard clay earth" beneath the stones. Earlier in the piece, the land is said to be filled with treasure, and earlier still, digging through clay is compared to speaking, finding starlight, connection, origins. The poem was written after doing research on the Thai-Burmese border in 1996 and 1997, visiting refugee and military camps, becoming close to and collecting the stories of men and women who had been incarcerated in Burmese prisons. This time was crucial for me, a new kind of education, but it was also exhausting and sometimes traumatic.

No matter how huge the gaps in situation and experience, it is inevitable and necessary that we understand both the woundedness and the resilience of others through our own bodies. The despair I experienced on the border brought me full-circle, in an unnerving, uncontrollable way, to a dark place very similar to the one I had known as a small child. After the border, I returned to rural Greece, as I have returned there for a decade, to heal myself.

Iatre, therapefson seafton. Physician, heal thyself. The words are ancient Greek, spoken by Jesus, rather ironically, in the book of Luke. But even today, testifying to the strong link between the tongue and history, a Greek peasant would understand these words. I have heard the phrase spoken, also ironically, by friends taking their first sip of coffee after a night of over-indulgence. *The Disorder of Love* is a book about love in various forms, as obsession, as chaos and lust, as gift and refuge, and as healing, too, particularly when it comes in the strange form of finding a home, a centre, in a foreign country among foreign people.

It is not so surprising for a Canadian, born in a country built of so many different nations and voices, to choose to enter other landscapes and languages, to become a foreigner by choice. It is impossible to separate the history of my era—this post-industrial, migrant-filled, technologically-charged time—from that of my family. Though my initial departure was a well-timed escape, it has always been important for me to be going towards as well: education and experience in the world, wisdom in more than one dialect, spirit in more than one religion, laughter in all of it.

Very early in my work, I named my family as "the other," and did not want to be like them, or to become them. Then I spent the next fifteen years searching out the other, giving myself passionately to other countries and other languages. I am the other now; and I am, at long last, part of my own family again. As an evolving anti-nation like Canada suggests most ably, the other is ourselves.

More and more people in the world no longer live in the countries where they were born. Any Canadian city—increasingly, any city on the planet—is a loud proclamation about how strangers make homes and build lives out of the materials and the landscape at hand. It is possible for people to maintain connections to their countries of origin while becoming neighbours with others very unlike (and very like) themselves.

Writing this, I falter, pausing, casting about for words. I am aware both of the over-simplifications and of the real pain involved in this "one world as home" stance, particularly for those people who are forced to leave their countries because of violent political and economic upheaval. In Canada, racism and discrimination are much more prevalent than some people think—particularly those who are unlikely to suffer it—and race-related violence continually haunts our past and violates our present.

Though living elsewhere is more common now than it has ever been before, living far from home is still not easy.

Departures involve choices that are understood only later to be immense sacrifices, despite all the apparent gains, and to make a home in one place precludes having the same kind of home in another. In Greek, as in English and French and Spanish, we talk about setting down roots. When you buy a house in Greece, people say, *Kalo riziko*: good roots, meaning, may you grow strong roots here, a family of your own.

To say the words out loud, *Kalo riziko*, causes a physical response, a corresponding echo, in my stomach. Yet I write this in a very unrooted place full of urban transients, Vancouver, a spectacularly beautiful, peculiarly clean city with little history and less active memory. Though gardens grow like jungles here, my few plants live in pots. Someone else is watering my olive trees on the island. I have just arrived here from somewhere else; half of my belongings are still in boxes, on the other side of deep water.

To be split, as I feel split, between cultures, languages, countries, loyalties, is to nurse a curious, long-term fracture. It does not leave you, cannot, because it has become you. All of us are fragmented in more or less perceptible ways; many people have more than one language, one home, one allegiance, one truth. As confusing as that fragmentation and multiplicity can be, they also offer us a new way to understand our world and to approach the work of being engaged human beings. Though the poet healed herself by discovering a home in Greece, the disorder of love was not so neatly unravelled. By its very nature, it never will be. Slowly, wherever I live, I learn to find a peace within the complexity of what I am, what I was, what I am becoming.

The woman named Voula, who is the subject of the last poem in this book, was a wild person when I knew her, and tended to drive other people wild, too. Yet when I wrote just now of finding peace, her face appeared in my mind.

Voula often reminded me, and reminds still, of the last line in a long poem by Seferis: *We who had nothing shall teach them peace.*

When this battle-scarred woman danced, she was home, at peace. In the last poem, she dances to the music of *rebetiko* in the village square, taking a traditionally male dance and turning it into an act of seduction and celebration for the women she loves, women who were watching and admiring her that night, and dancing around her. To her friends, she repeatedly cried out two well-loved phrases which sound almost like benedictions, *Na zeseis hilia kronia, na zezeis panda!*

I was there, too, with Greek friends both male and female, and one of the men, another writer, asked a question meant to be rhetorical: Why was Voula allowed to dance at all? then he cursed her. Voices rising above the bouzoukia and the accordion, the two of us got into a brief but serious argument. I abruptly left the table and stalked off. That night I wrote Voula's poem, hoping to answer my friend's ugliness with language that revealed the beauty, the power, and the generosity of her dance.

Later that year, she left the island after a group of village men beat her up outside a café. No one in our circle of common friends and acquaintances has seen her since. Wherever Voula is, I pray the world has taken care of her. She taught me much about the disorder, and the abiding order, of love.

THE SMALL WORDS
IN MY BODY

~

For it is not right that in the house of song there
be mourning. Such things befit not us.

—Sappho, after the
death of her daughter,
7th Century B.C.

PART ONE

Four Suites

THE REMARKABLE CHEAPNESS

OF BLOOD

I keep a picture
        of him
        as a little boy
Black and white but
his eyes were green then,
        I can tell by the way
        he is laughing,
                his mouth full of spring,
                        marbles, flawless teeth

I can tell by the way
the grass in the background
        is the same shade of light as his eyes
        and the sky is related to this colour
                that shines
                and shines

He learned the intricacies
        of catching frogs that summer,
                the different feel of frog skin, grass, mud
He became an artist at swimming,
                        fighting,
                            swearing,
                    running the entire length of the field
                    where the ponies grazed
                    beside the stone-scattered stream

I know all this by one
    coffee-ringed photograph
He never had to explain anything to me
I know he did not really spend
    his first twelve years slaughtering
        pigs and horses

Nor did he skin living rabbits
His eyes are no longer green
because green is the colour
    we learn to kill

(The grassy background of the photo has
    been smothered in concrete
        for twenty years)

HOUSES DOWN

From three houses down comes
a child's wail: a splinter slipped
under a fingernail, some stolen food, death.
It is difficult to know.
The real is here, truth like fish-hooks
in my people's skin.
These are not stories but days.

Mud licks at the ankles
after long rains.
The small details:
      a paper cut that gnaws the knuckle,
      the thin fierce cats eating garbage.
In the alley, the matted skeleton of a small bird
        sleeps among the stones.
Crows screech dark songs.

Rain for days but we will not drown.
The sun will arrive on time.
It will rub against his eyelids,
      make promises about the daylight
        which he will believe.

From My Father's Hand

In the pockets
I find horses' hair,
the sleek fur of a pussy willow,
old keys.

I reach into that house
    and pull out the painful creak
    of the stairs.
I find a ruined painting on a water-stained wall,
    a photograph too old to be real.
In the bottom of a drawer
there is a poem by Alexander
    —*All creatures great and small*—
        and finally I have to laugh at that.

All these things
lie about you.
They mutter dreams to me,
words I never heard you say.
You shot the grey-hooved pony,
    axed away marsh willows.
Your keys always shone like polished copper,
      cold in my hands,
      bright as blood.

Can it be you spent
    your whole life
    killing what you didn't mean to?
The wind does not
    blow the truth into my hair.
    Nothing is that easy.

But if you did live
        by drawing death,
        who and what am I?
Splinters of spruce and bone
        fester in my skin,
        slivers of the questions
        I carve in this house
                where you lived.

And here is one more, with my apologies
        tacked on like a crimson target:
                Why do I use the house, the dusty pocket,
                the past tense as if you were dead and I
                am suffering some warped sorrow?

You are there, in the field, walking home.
The red sun cuts over your head like a knife.
A clean rifle is slung over your shoulder
        and a doe rabbit hangs from your fist
                by thin silk ears.
Her blood touches your leg like a hand.

The Fifth Season
for Michael Ondaatje

Words off his tongue
    like painted wind,
    words that catch the mind
        as hands catch water,
            spilling light.
It is words I dream at night,
    stories from the black and white,
        legends, commandments.
I have asked for a compass,
    even slightly damaged,
    for journeys against the dark.

What do I remember?
What do I know?
There are four seasons
    and a fifth that some learn.
The season of refusal,
    it does not turn leaf to autumn.

Leaves furl back to buds.
Branches curl up like crushed hands
    and the trees themselves
    heave slowly into the ground.
Even the grass razors backwards
        and disappears,
        sharply, an orchestrated movement,
            as if the earth has suddenly
            inhaled its landscape.
Dirt rubs sky on every horizon.

This is the fifth season,
      when history is gone
      and words have neither
          echoes nor meanings
When my father is lost
      and my sister rots alone.

This is the season where I live
      with a poisoned dog.
This season is the song of those people
         who did not learn words.
They woke darkened by mud, naked,
         driven by nightmares.
They ate earth, leaves, sunlight.
I was born here, am part of a place
      I cannot understand
      but cannot abandon,
      which is almost love.

In other seasons,
      men with practical blue eyes
         and civilized accents
         speak and read out loud.
In other seasons, poplar leaves blow
      down the gutters
      like spilled yellow paint.
Fathers watch their children grow
         beautiful in autumn.
They keep stories in small silver boxes
         with old leaves, autumn leaves scented,
            always, by wind.

FAMILY REUNIONS

The other people quit their stone fields to come here.
They slip in from nights that even the snow abandons.
They leave ashes in their glasses and stains on the table.
The house is littered with bits of their hair and skin.
Bones clatter through the holes in their pockets.

Their hands scythe down the light.
They dance their words to bloody stumps.
They bite the world and spit it out on the table,
        bitter, determined only to dirty
        every glass in these cupboards
        and break at least three.

Rage keeps them awake until night opens to dawn
                    gently, like a woman's hands.
Then they unfold the worn quilts of their lives
But their skeletons do not soften in sleep.

On waking, they are sad and broken.
They drink coffee with tongues swollen by talk and grief.
During breakfast, they seed the floor with sugar
        and spill the milk, complain the toast
                is never warm enough.
When they leave, they walk like shadows
        who have lost their bodies to wolves.

They are the people from a history I've forgotten.
I ignore mirrors and cut my hair.
I bleach my eyes white
        to blind the other inside of me.
I wash every glass carefully,
        with a soft cloth,
        breaking nothing.

ANNIE'S BOY
for David

She says: At night, I lock that door
            and lie awake wondering,
            Suppose he gets in?

Why do you fear the little boy?

            Because he can pick a lock.
            At thirteen, his hands are bigger than mine.
            Something beats against his skull in the dark.
            I've watched him nearly tear his jaws in songs
                  I cannot understand.
            I've seen him skin squirrels, smiling to do it.

            To watch him run away
            is to know he could run towards
                  just that fast,
            his fists like weights against his ribs,
            his legs like axes swinging at the ground.

Then Annie's quiet.
She stares at the stove.
She drags a rag across her knuckles.
She cuts the thread of her mouth
      to a smile, to a laugh.
            What do you expect?
            The rugs are not tacked down.
            The screens are frayed and who can tell
                  what lives under the floorboards?
            Some huge snake has curled to sleep
                  in the pipes of this house,
                  flooding each room.
            Mornings, wind rattles my finger bones.

I drop frying pans and coffee pots,
        make neighbours complain of noise.
The dogs in the alley howl,
        the crag-shouldered cats
        fight under the steps.
What do you expect?

        His bones are a cage he prowls around.
        Once, I found one of those cats on my porch,
                its neck cracked
                like a thin twist of copper
                its shock-green eyes open wide.

LUNCH IN THE CITY

We are not in the forest.
There are no guns under the bed now,
    no wolf threats, no axe-bladed animal nights.
This is the gleaming city
        where the gravel is false
        and salty over ice.
There is no muffled silence of snow here,
    no trees or traplines or
    impossible deep distances to run.
This is the city where I live.
The only tracks behind me are my own.

Look at the reflection in the windows.
Of course I belong here.
It's your boots and broken-ice face
    that melt in the reek of exhaust.
Your drunk hands fumble
    with parking meters and restaurant bills.
You can barely read the street signs.

But even the vagabond cells, on touching,
        will pulse together.
Your heart beats a steady chaos,
        a red cacophony of past.
When I meet you on the street, my eyes blur.
For a long moment, I am blind.
My hands disappear.
The air becomes too thick—
    I flop on the sidewalk
    with gills of shredded silk.
Even in winter, I can smell mud and moss.
I can touch the bits of flesh twisting underground.
Worms bitten by your shovel squirm a last dance in my limbs.

For lunch, no, I'm not very hungry
But we toss them around,
        pieces of expensive meat.
You chew the skeleton clean.
I don't have to see to remember.
Don't waste anything if you can use it, you said.

I'm not wasted.
I have good clothes, Father,
        my nails are long, my fingers
        were never tapered but there's nothing wrong
                with this skin,
                whatever I touch, I can feel.
My shoes make a sharp noise in the hallways,
                my spine is buttoned straight.
You can hardly make a right angle
        with your bones now,
        even your fingers curl, forgetful.
You lean over to hear my voice,
                nearly old,
                nearly something else.
You scarcely recall knives and forks.

But I remember well.
Don't get old.
I can't afford you pity now.
Don't let your face shrivel to sleep
                before I learn to hate it
                and bait its hooks
                with all the rotten skin I've shed for you.

Weary of that colour,
    of these words sifted onto paper,
        worried over like fine gold dust.

This is the last.
Then I graduate from these bitter stories.
Long ago I left you sleeping in a hallway,
    a dismantled scarecrow in an empty house,
        your face oddly pale,
        bloodless as a puppet's.

But I remember the living coil of colour
    snaking up and out of you.
A good man you were,
    gave blood twice a year.
The nurse's hair slid like egg yolk
        from her white cap.
There's nothing more generous
        than donating, she said
        while you wrung the rag
        of your arm into the needles
Who did you save by bleeding yourself?

The living things always needed gutting,
    your own body, even mine.
Love was the red lesson once,
    then again and again,
    pain I learned to sing
    with my eyes closed.

Every year skinned deer
        hung like blankets from the rafters.
Behind their erased skins,
        maps shone blue and red,
        river after river, whole countries
            of blood to move through.

Here, you said, *put your hand here*
And flesh like marble
        warmed by sunlight
        licked my fingers.

Oh, to abandon every simple cleanness
            to my lessons.
Unable to believe in stories
or the heaven of animals:
the summer of shooting the dog
        was a grand season of study.
One silver and black shot.
Three ragged yelps across the green air
And a silence slammed together
        like two rocks in a boy's hands.
It is still here, deadbolted over my head.

A good man though.
You owned a strange honesty.
No sin in showing me mousetraps,
dead rabbits, torn-winged birds, etc.
You taught me the one truth you understood:
        the remarkable cheapness of all blood,
            even my own.

Now I should cry thank you.
I should be glad.

GRAVE DIGGING

for Tracy Lynn Connelly,
April 12, 1960–July 31, 1984

How Clean You Have Become

Slowly, I learn the power
    of forgetfulness,
    of blindness
    of closing my eyes
        to whisper pretty stories
            to myself in the dark, alone.

In the end, the edges of memory
        are licked smooth
            by the rough tongue of time,
              wiped clean.
All you did was beautiful, and good.

There is a backwards slip in evolution.
I am a salamander in a deep cave.
My sunless skin breathes
    cell by cell
    over my eyes.

All you did was beautiful.
With death comes love,
    strange partners in a hard dance,
        but you sway perfectly.
You are a graceful angel,
    a good devil,
    a woman without sins or scars,
        held perfectly
        still in the teeth of cameras,
            smiling.

I do not recall.
I do not call home the lost blood.
Your death is a dream
    I wake from, forgetful.
With the downward slide of days,
    how clean you have become,
        how lovely.

Out of time and darkness
　　　and dreams of her,
　　　　　I wake to the grey hands
　　　　　of dawn holding me.
This winded night, blood has blown through my body,
　　　slamming every door and window
　　　in my chest.
She left before sunlight, her face blurred.

Today, the sun burns the clouds.
It is spring again, a year closer to dying.
I'd meant to find good words for the new season.
But where is she?

I was too small to turn on the lights.
I could not reach the switch.
There was no colour in our parting.
The curve of her cheek looped
　　　around and around in my eyes.
Wind swallowed her hair
　　　when she opened the door.

The memory is black and white.
It is really an old photograph,
　　　an echoing shot, another daybreak.
I am confused, still the child
　　　　　stretching a thin arm up the wall,
　　　　　unable to reach the light.
Has someone cut off my fingers?

There are no answers
        to the questions
        of dreams at dawn.
That shuddering I hear in my chest
            is neither an answer
            nor the nerves of love.

No, it is not love.
It is my heart
It is my heart
It is my heart
slamming doors.

Will dry bones clatter to the floor?
Will her eyes crack and shatter?
Her hands wriggle with blue worms,
        the fingers mesh together, shrunken,
                knuckles like marbles
                sewn under the skin.

There are footnotes
at the bottom of every page,
                a dead pigeon on the sidewalk,
                an old lady on the train.

Every day the trains run back and forth.
Their people stare through sullen eyes.
The sun is trapped under the earth.
There are no songs, no pretty stones
        stirred in among the gravel.
Somewhere, even children rot.

Today I cannot be calm.
I cannot forget.
The air is burlap
        on my skin,
                against my tongue.

Birdsong

Birds blind to glass
　　　are classic:
　　　　　they fly hard,
　　　　　arc wings windward, effortless—
　　　　　　then slip stunned
　　　　　　　　down the windows.

How many times did we do this?
They laughed at the two of us
　　　when we screeched and danced
　　　on the front lawn.
Someone waved.
They thought we were singing.

We were the ugliest crows.
We were magpies
　　　who reigned in the alleys
　　　in the ravines between houses.
We were mute birds, not songbirds.
Gentle music bit our ears like ticks.

But dear sister, you are finally learning to sing.
The bones of birds are hollow.
Your ribs, played by wind, whistle high silver songs.

Now I live in our nest alone.
I pick through this clutch of feather and bone.
How do birds mourn?
When I cry, they think I am singing.

GRAVE DIGGING

I study all the magic.
I listen to Gregorian chants.
I think of Job, who said
    I do repent in dust and ashes
        and make a retraction.
I take back the silence I gave you.
I tear my clothes and fast.

Even black spells, I read them
    upside-down, every pagan word.
In the dark, inside a red star,
I turn three times and catch wind-streams
       in my hair, kill a white cat.
Honey and pig's blood,
    rabbit's teeth and shavings of tin.

How shall I conjure you back to life?
You lived alone with your back to life,
    danced alone in a place
    I search for even now.
I go outside of my mind
    with a scrap of your clothes
       in my hand, a ravelling talisman.
I call and call.
What if I get lost out here,
    cannot find my way back in?
Isn't that what happens?

If I had your bones in a bag,
Then I would know you are dead.
That rattle beside me would be a song.
I wish I had to carry your bones
        wherever I went.

If I had to dig your grave,
Then I would believe you are dead.
I could lick the dirt from my fingers
        or toss it on your head.
A grave is a hole in the heart.
It can only mean one thing.
I want to dig that hole.

The ancient tribes ate their dying
        to keep them alive.
It has worked well for Christ.
I will try it. I will try anything.

Where is your body?

Where are you?

Where?

WHY PEOPLE HAVE LOVERS NOW

It's Easy For the Men I Know

The private apocalypse is an option chosen by some.
I test myself and periodically walk in front of cars.
Death, too, can be a desire, a hunger,
    a whine, what you're really looking for
    when you fuck those men.
Orion howls and heaves down his spear.
The trees sneer through the glass.

They tell me not to dwell on these things.
Orion hunts far away.
The trees do not have hands that can crush you.
The trees are not alive.
Sorrow is temporary, they say.

I accept the dirty notes they give to me.
I turn my hate into compromise, my tears
    into a day by the river.
I slide into the clean waters,
        trail my hands in the reflected sky,
        pretend to see heaven wash around me.

They see my face when the wind tears
    off the water, pulls the hair away.
I turn my head, smile.
I wear a well-melted mask of thick plastic for them.
I wear a doll's stupid, beautiful face.

And it's easy for them to lay me down:
    they think my clicking lids
    drop tight against the dark.

WHY PEOPLE HAVE LOVERS NOW

It's the nights, darkness,
    the dreams I live for,
    a child's scope,
I see the sweet in everything:
        ants dance between the stones,
        rainbows of oil twist down the gutters,
        a girl gets balloons, balloons,
            black kittens.

When I wake, I remind myself
the sun is a coincidence,
    only a star closer than the others.
Mornings offer thirsty roaches on the facecloth.
The day falls down as I plan my night's dreams.

Sometimes, I know they will fail,
        corner me and draw sweat,
        leave me wrung and tired
          of waking.
I arrange for those dreams accordingly.

That is why people have lovers now.
After nightmares we wake
    to stranger's skin
    mistaken life
        a bonfire of flesh
        to burn the bad dreams down.

Simple, what you're looking for:
     a cheap skull so close you can't see it,
          so close your eyes blur and you close them.
You need a hard double trail of arms
        leading to a plain of skin,
          a man's back.

You want muscle in his chest
      and above his collarbones,
         warm flesh to breathe life into your hands.
It's been done before with clay.

You want to beg the innocent men passing
      in the street for this.
They wear chiselled faces
      and suits that equal three months' rent.
At night, reading your first book, you think:
      Is it possible?
      Was I forgotten?
      Why didn't I get a rib?

Simple, finding it,
      simple as rain on a cat's skeleton,
      these touches that bleach sinew to white thread.
You find the hands and the arms
      and the long strong torso
         with your eyes closed.
The breath from the buried lungs touches your tongue.
But you need the bones underneath.

Nobody's willing to give those up.
They pretend they're asleep if you mention it.
Or, like Adam in the original edition, they say,

What do you mean, one of my ribs?

In the morning, if you stay, they call you crazy
and ask if you talk in your sleep.

THE BEAUTIFUL JOKE

The mime face
your mask of quiet
calm as rain slipping away
        beading down the window
                on the other side of white-gloved hands
You are an artist, skilled
perhaps invisible

Pantomime
An act:
you standing kind and silent at the glass
sloped grey eyes split with black
your back a curve, a cradle
        created by my hands
your face flung open like a dream on waking

This is all
a pantomime
(Jokes like everything else
        contain beauty)
Behind your white mask
        a storm screams

I may not see it
        Blindness is a way of life
But I feel it on the ridge of my shoulders
                the bite of hail
                        on my lips
                the rain tears into my ears,
                        deeper, down
                                down my throat.

When I Became Another Animal

I begin as a cat in the crook
    of your knees, curled and purring.
This is my body, in the morning,
    painted with autumn's cold light.

I bring you
        the good gift of cats:
            animals small, still warm,
              brightly laced with blood and fur.
I bring you ravens,
        their wings white with night-frost.
I give you lives and slips of torn skin, anyone's.

In time, I become another animal.
I grow, stretch out in a naked skin.
My new fingers clutch sheets.
We sleep together at night
    but I cannot stare down
        darkness now.
We do not see each other.
This blindness
        makes touching
        possible.

When you turn towards,
    your mouth on me
        is like salt on a cut.
Your body, a blade to carve me to bone.
I am a soft stone of flesh.

It is my fault, my affliction.
I've let myself be shorn.
And I make it a gift,
    give you life,
    slips of torn skin,
        mine.

A Moth in a Glass

A trapped heart thumps at the lid of my mouth.
My heart does not remember this place.

You have waited for me
And when I appear, it is nothing
             magical.
There is no laughter or clapping
    or flapping white doves.

I am gathered like new grass cuttings
      in your arms, fresh and almost alive.
There is bribery with the hands,
         washing skin raw.
Nerves jump and shudder like live wires in rain.
This touching is safety, is love, is forgiveness.
Then you sleep.

Somewhere past this night,
      daylight breaks open, crashes on the rocks
         of an ocean I've abandoned.

I watch you sleep.
My heart batters against me
      like a moth in a glass.
It cannot believe it lives here.
I curl out of the hollows of your body.
My cold hands hold each other perfectly.

But it's true, from a distance, if anyone saw us,
They would think we must be touching.

A Nightmare and a True Story

This is a nightmare:
innocent as a dog,
skin that sleek, pink-tongued,
dumb as a dog,
I follow you into the white light.
I pad faithful behind you, leap up
onto the table and wag my entire body.
I am oblivious to silver-edged scalpels.

This is the beautiful stupidity of dogs.

A needle in the proper place.
My shining fur turns to water.
Something slips through my skin
    like a finger through dust.
The painlessness is part of the nightmare.

I cannot see it but I know it
    —dreams are like that—
Across the room
there is a large glass cylinder.
Two fine strands stretch down.
They suspend a heart beating in Ringer's solution.
The heart thumps on the counter,
    closes, opens valves like blinking eyes.
I am laid on the table, hollow,
    ribs snapped open clean as shells.

The heart is wet, a full flower after rain.
It mutters to itself, tells ridiculous stories
              over and over.
Eventually you grow bored,
admit it to the silence of a jar.

II

Not her heart.
The truth is, hands.
She had hands, five fingers each,
      betraying her true species.
Her hands held you, held roses,
      wrote letters, wrote the best words
      on your very human skin.

Now they are gone, lost,
      pickled or sold or glassed into paperweights.
Without them, she never speaks.
Her fingers were tongues.

THE SMALL WORDS IN MY BODY

Believer I am, but admit it:
     words will not cure everything.
Breathless unless in the mouth,
     on a page, they are crushed spiders.
They have nothing
     to do with the details
     that make a life.
Every language is different and none exact.

Close the books then.
They cannot cure this.
On the shelf they clench
each other, spines rigid with silence.

I am tough leather.
I am buckets of blood and bone.
They are my own.
There's no way to drain or erase
        myself.

Openings do not close.
My blood writes a story
I cannot believe.

Lying in white sheets,
     I sharpen my scissors,
    and select a knife.
        I clip and slice
        the small words from here.

The splitting cells,
      the tale whispering in my blood
          cannot protest
          but cuts to silence.
I scrape out the scrawl, this mistake.

As with the gentlest nightmare,
I forget just as I wake.

CAREFULLY, YOU KILL

There was a broken bone under my skin.
I wanted to keep that limb
    and its clawed hand.
The body's memories persist:
        a phantom movement,
          muscles flex and throw,
          strength runs down my shoulder
            like an ant, quick and red.

But my mind laughs.
The arm is gone.
The hand is buried and the fingers
    claw dirt
    in a deep place.
At night I dream I dance with you.
But the daily task is a slow killing,
    piece by piece, one touch
    at a time and blood blooms on my skin.
Carefully, lovingly, killing, an act
      with its own science.

This is a room in your house,
  in a hospital.
The walls are square and white.
You do not believe in flowers or photographs.
Nothing is hidden.
The smell of you sleeps in the sheets.

How easily that once happened.
I remember you beautiful.
I remember two bodies braided here.

Where is that flesh,
    that coil of muscle and whisper?
I want to find some part of us whole,
      still clean,
         alive,
           with every finger
              attached.

The strange bright creature
that lived between us is dead.
We admit nothing
but perform the autopsy together,
    silent doctors without tongues,
      embarrassed by the crippled words
         we would make.
We pull away, uncover.
Objective eyes peer inside.
I nod.
No tears fall between the contracted ribs.
We dissect.

We peel ourselves apart with gloved fingers,
not hesitant but just a blink away
      from disgust.
Skin and certain bones are missing.

Finished, we toss the remains
to the backs of our minds,
    to those fields scattered
    with a great many bones.
The birds appear, great glistening blacks,
    loose-jawed dogs lope up,
    beetles with red shells soldier in,
      hungry.
You refuse to witness this.
You scrub your fingernails.

I stay, sit on a sun-bleached skull,
    pleased with how quickly,
      how cleanly the animals work,
      pleased with the beauty of scavengers.

THE GOOD AND GENTLE LIES

The words exist only in our language.

In other countries, they are the songs of lost birds.
The skin of these words will melt in the ocean
      between the teeth of salt and sand.
Late, late at night, I see them
      drifting about you in blue darkness,
          smaller than you know,
          dusted silver like moths.

They are the gentlest songs:
      yours is the last quilt of skin
      I will hold against my body
          yours are the last eyes I will see
      yours, the only hands
          you, the last truth I will find,
            the last I will need.

I do not believe it now,
      but the words are lies.
We tell ourselves this is the last skin
          to make us into the creature we dream at night,
            but we know that animal lives
              in a land we fear.
When we love, we love sadly, wild,
      like a long storm that will not break.

Later, we turn our backs.
We kiss our walls.
We touch the velvet eyes of sleep.
I turn away, as if your body were made of scarred wood,
          as if your heart were not inside it,
          but lost outside at night,
           a nameless sparrow.

LANGUAGES I HAVE FAILED TO LEARN

LANGUAGES I HAVE FAILED TO LEARN

There is a language between the trees and the sky.
To learn it now is impossible.
The edges touching each other,
    the cross-hatching against dawn-light:
        these are secrets.

At night, you walk on frost-killed grass.
You have nowhere to go.
Don't cry, you are not
        a cat begging love.
    Don't screech at the moon, it will not
        understand.
    Stop it, your mother might say,
        or she might join you.
Anyone can see you out here in this field.
From their houses across the way,
    you are a broken dancer in the dark.
    Shhh. Shhh.
They think you are crazy
    when you dance
    when you dare to sing songs
        in your language.

You've failed the other languages.
Why can't you make the letters?
Are your fingers broken?
    Or is it your mind?
Something in you is flawed.

When you refused to cut
    into the white belly
        of a mouse
    the small scientist
    with small eyes asked,
Do you have a crippled tongue?

Your brain could not breathe.
It ran backwards, it tripped,
        its wrinkles unwound, it rolled away
                like a ball of yarn.
You could not understand the little man
        or the bags and bags of wet mice.
You couldn't say a word.
What a foolish girl.

There is also a language
        between carcasses and sharp instruments
        between little men and slips of pickled blood.
When sheeps' eyes came to class
        like some foreign delicacy,
        you cut your finger with a scalpel
        and were excused.

Language. The words.
Life in a brick cave,
        waking hours in libraries
        and yellow rooms lined with textbooks.

Even with chalk-dust in your nose
                you remained dumb.

Outside the trees and sky touched.
In the winds, they danced, sang,
        spoke to each other
        in a language you almost understood,
        remembered, almost,
                even through the panes
                of glass.

I Am One of the Privileged

I.

One tragedy after another, great or small, mostly small, but they feel great, they *feel*; that's the catch. This life, this hand playing the muscles of a back, touching the thinnest skin of lips and eyelids—it feels original, a new story that must end well or you will die, you will not survive another miserable ending.

But you do. The man, who is a construction worder, bends with a shovel. As his back curves, something high above him shifts, not the moon or the stars, nothing that huge but something else, a block of metal left in the wrong place by someone who has corned beef waiting for him at lunch. Suppose it had been merely peanut butter and jam? If there had been more sunlight, less wind? Speculation is pointless. The equations of chance cannot be untangled by even the most skilled mathematician. The variables are too numerous, and hidden, like the brittle trap of bones in an old man's hand.

As his back curves, something breaks off the skeleton of a building, something falls out of the sky, not the moon or the stars but a shard of metal. And his back is crushed, that fine-muscled back coated with a skin like cream chocolate. And his lips, when his body catapults forward, are ground into the gravel.

It is almost like a laboratory experiment, the precision of it, the clean hit. It is a laboratory experiment, in fact. In any reputable university, they'll do this with kittens, drop a lead weight on their spines and later assess the damages. This is tragic, too, despite the cheapness of kittens, and even if you don't like cats.

II.

That's the secret God knows, the one we touch all our lives but never recognize. We are not born blind but we don't know how to see either. We are always saying, "What, what? What was that?" Like surprised dogs, we whip our heads back and forth. That is what a poem is, that convulsive double twist at the neck when tragedy happens, that sincere scribble of questions disguised as similes, metaphors, and, in high school, onomatopoeia, a word I could never spell, though I knew what 'sobbing' sounded like.

The secret is in kittens, wandering shrews, horses, and dew worms, the ones in the garden that you never fail to cut in half with the shovel. Let's call a spade a spade, shall we? It's remarkable, but it's true: it does not matter how much we love our lives. Someone is always in the goddamn garden, turning up the soil and eventually you go down, sliced in the middle, or maybe just across the legs. It may be an accident: the woman who shoots her own husband, imagining a thief. Every summer, farmers' sons lose pieces of their lives to thick blades near hay and sawdust. For horses, it is gopher holes and odd bone diseases, then slaughter houses, dogfood, or a trip overseas to a European delicatessen.

Why don't we eat horses?

God would eat horses. If God were hungry, he would eat anything. He does.

III.

But I am one of the privileged, to have the fingers to write this.
I am one of the lucky who stares appalled at the world, then eats
cheesecake. In my family, when people die, we generally know
where the body is, and there are good funerals. Think of all the
idiots' cafés, the homes of argument over Lebanon and liver and
onions, over cheap psychology and the mating habits of
intellectuals. If you have eyes for the newspaper in the morning,
the world tears open like a dog shot with a rifle.

Newspapers are undisguised poetry, tragedy straight-up for those
addicted to sorrow. Some will shoot water into their veins just for
that cool rush—you will read even the classified ads after the
stories of torture in Chile and New York.

Yes, I've seen beauty, too, flowers and mountains and puppies and
the deep blue sky, it's all there in abundance and, like a popular
joke, the sun keeps rising. I'm a happy person when I don't wear
my glasses. Unable to read the fine print or see past the edge of a
clean porcelain bathtub, the world is Eden to me. Some days I
purposefully walk about half-blind to bask in the blur, in the
softness of things seen without sharp edges.

But there are only so many walls I will waltz into before that need
catches up with me, that hunger, the weakness for words and
sight, for truth more blinding than sunlight after a curtained
hour of skin. A library is a gallery of horrors, those weak-spined
books of poetry, those poems that dance tragedy to life, that
wring beauty from the savage. If it's self-indulgent, all the better.
Who else can we indulge besides ourselves? Who else is there,
when we can save nothing but our own skins?

IV.

Once over the danger of the ocean, I stumbled my way across a
continent like a monk chanting out of key, a pilgrim tripping in
long robes. After dreams of saving something, anything duller
than the light of God, I woke to the scurry of sun-oiled
cockroaches. In India, fathers break their children's legs to make
them better beggars. This is great poetry, the sound of
eight-year-old bones cracking. It is onomatopoeic, it says
everything in seconds, it is Shakespearean in its power.

But how embarrassing. It was too much for me, that crackling
song; my veins nearly burst with the rush, I couldn't breathe. The
most noble aspiration I had was to vomit. I could only look away
and hurry deeper into the slum of brilliant colour, bolts of blue
cloth, hen's blood, thin brown faces beautiful and sullen and
secret.

The April Nightmares

Woe to whoever commences his life without lunacy.
                                          —Kanzantzakis

I

I am awake
but my eyes are closed.
Witches (not angels)
are slipping bodily
out of the stains on my ceiling.
They are dangerous creatures.
Despite my eyelids, I see them very clearly.
They go through skin like needles.
I cannot move when they are here.
My tongue becomes a heavy blind leech.
I cannot speak.
I concentrate on breathing.

They are shrivelled dolls,
        dolls with singed heads,
        pressing close,
        but never touching,
        not quite.
I hear their laughter riddled
through the night.
It works into me like woodworm,
        then spreads.

My mind spits at all my muscles,
but they remain dry,
stuck to their bones.
I listen to the crones
cackling, laughing
      so loud I clench my teeth.
Their voices shake me, break
me in the mind.
It is close
to rape
some savagery
without definition.
Only the skin knows
and cries.

Then they fade.
They suck themselves away
like retreating wind.
Liquid seeps back into my lips.
I can open my mouth.
I can shift my hips.
I am alive.
I am awake
(but I was never asleep)
and the witches are gone
(back into the stains).

I rise and open the windows
(the world is still there).
I conceive the idea
of 'breakfast',
watch the water boil,
smell tea, feel the steam
kiss my face.
I eat a green apple,
        noisily, like a horse.
The sink is bright as a jewel,
the counter whiter than God.
I know witches don't exist.

I examine my wrist
        rising into my arm.
I touch my neck,
        my face.
I am here, in my kitchen.
Sunlight drips
out of the silver taps.
The glasses are kindled with water.

I am not lost.
I am present.
I am accounted for.
I am.

II

In the dream, there is nothing
        but a grid,
        a thin brush,
        a bit of grey paint.
I watch the brush lick lightly
at the paper,
fill in the grid at random,
slowly, poke the squares
        into greyness,
        a tone for overcoats,
        sick skin, animal fur,
        winter slush, pavement

(Pavement: the streets of the city,
  lives pressed
  brittle as flowers in old books.
The streets, where people walk quickly
  because they are dying,
  touching nothing
  beyond their grey hands,
  hearts, grey, folded
        in briefcases
        and hat boxes.
On the pavement, we clutch
our knuckles like marbles,
sad and vicious children
waiting to play a game
  in the dirt.)

In the grey dream, the grid
shadows in, shades away
square by square,
not a life or death colour
but the tone of nothing,
 a throb so constant
 it is no longer felt.

This is the silent nightmare,
no shrieks or heartbeats,
no cackles, not a single word.
Words are smothered.

This drab painting
is a nightmare
because I know
the grid means my mind.
I can see my brain
 flood with the licks
 of the little black brush.

When I wake, it does not stop.
The brush flicks on,
 cool and tongued
 like a snake.

III

Not a nightmare
but a mirage in my skull:

walking naked in the rain
in a high green country.

I learn to live
with my face to the face
of the mountain.

I listen to the words of stones,
whisper secrets to veins of gold
and granite ears.

I live in a cage of stars.
I stare out of the Dog's mouth,
dance on the edge of the Crown,
slide down Orion's silver ankles.

        They call,

       Come down
           come away
                come home
                     they say

They stand in doorways,
fingers sharp as pencils,
teeth like nickels,
eyes like dimes,
glittering,
teasing the jackdaws and crows.

I spit all their words
out of my mouth.
I walk through trees,
not doors.
I drown
in light and shadow
and wind.

PART TWO

LEARNING COLOUR AND DEMONS
NORTHERN THAILAND

To be born with the power of words is to
be born with an axe in your mouth.
Be very careful of the direction
in which you swing.

—A Buddhist proverb loosely
translated from the Thai

Learning Colour and Demons
Northern Thailand

I.

They tell me it is dangerous
     to walk into the fields at night.
The moon may be bright,
     but its clear face
     is not innocent.
It does not matter
     that you can see the stars better, they say.
Are you mad?

Where do you come from?
Fool, child, idiot.
You are white, not invisible.
They can see you, too.
Even better in the dark.

II.

In daylight the rice is greener than anyone's eyes,
Stands slender in sun-silvered water.
The sky is huge, deep, spills bright clouds
          just above your body.
Its blue edges touch you.
You stand on a red clay road, amazed,
     holding your breath to hear
     the snakes whisper away from you.

In the wagon ruts,
    the crushed shells of scorpions sleep black,
        five inches long.
But the land is safe.
The people smile at you
    with the faces of cats,
     clean-boned, beautiful,
        alive.

They touch your white arms,
Smile at your hair:
Gold, they say, and laugh.

There is no need for photographs.
All of this will exist forever,
    you could never forget
    the colour of the fields, their faces,
    these lives.
This is no dream.

III.

You don't understand,
Can't you see? they ask.
If only you could read our papers.
Your eyes are not dark enough.
This makes you blind.

If they offer you anything to drink,
Don't take it.
Thirst is easier than the thicker tongue of poison.

In your country, yes,
But here women do not choose freedom.
It is not universal.
Beginnings end at borders.
History is not a subject here, it owns you.
You live in its hand and it holds you still.

There is so much noise in the city, they say,
That no one hears screaming.
There are so many people,
Death-lists are never accurate.
Pieces of paper are lost, burned, or torn
        as easily as hair and skin.
Why do you believe everything?

IV.

They believe everything, the women
        of the fields.
You wash clothes with them,
Explain that machines can do this.
Laughing: what would we do then
                with white boxes thieving our work?

In Canada, they ask you,
Can you ever see the ghosts?
What do they look like?
You cannot answer.
You do have ghosts, though?
Yes, you tell them.

Here each family houses their ghosts
        in small temples of red and gold.
Ancestors are honoured with food,
        with wreaths of jasmine,
        with the flitting visits
          of sparrows and ants.
The people give their gentle demons
        a place to live.

At night, under a net as thin as shadow
You lie awake, trying to remember
        the ghosts in Canada:
                the shape of snowdrifts,
                the colour of stone,
                the sound of wind over ice.
Phantoms they could never feed.

v.

One hundred years ago,
It was law that the women
        who lied or spoke too loudly for too long
        were executed; not murder
                but correction.
Whipped to shreds, roasted, beaten to death
                with clubs carved of golden teak,
                or fed to alligators, or poisoned.
Whatever the methods, the result
                was silence.

It is not like that today.
Though it *is* possible to know too many words.
You might be learning too quickly.

VI.

You do learn quickly.
You cannot wake without some new knowledge,
            ants on your skin,
            a praying mantis on the bed,
            a frog in your shoe.
The mist glides into the village
            thick as cotton.
There are bells on the people's clothes.
The children teach you games with coins and stones.

You have never seen the grace of beauty
        that does not see itself.
Here it is everywhere; it slips
            sun-alive as water
                from the shoulders of the people.

At night, the lizards talk.
Cicadas ring a song clearer than silence.
Cats dance a staccato on the thin roof.

Before you never knew colours.
The darkness here is bright.
You sleep curled against skylight,
        prisms, wind-curved clouds.
Even in your dreams, you sing.

The Smallest Slaughter

In my country,
    spring arches its glossed back
    out of the ground.
Spring slips in among the stones
       and waits to splinter out sharp and green
       and alive.
Perhaps I should be home now,
    wrapped in the growing
    soft pelt of blue air.

It is dry season here.
The fields tear open,
    orange with fire.
Trees dance among the blowing red sheets.
Insects and birds batter against them, screaming.
Veins of smoke burst and bloody the sky for miles.
Then the fields uncurl gnarled as burned hands.

Dry season, it is the season of dying here
but my body plays a vicious joke.
My belly betrays me
    knows only spring
    sprouts a growth of cells.
A living cloth sews itself using my blood as thread.
It unravels me when I breathe.

No gentleness could be enough
so no gentleness at all.
A drawing-in begins now.
The wooden windows slam shut.
The frame bites the door.
Even the smallest slaughter
    demands a mourning of silence.

At night, two creatures hold
    the blade of darkness,
     waiting to be bled.
I do not sleep but dream awake
       of procedures, a hilltribe witch's eyes,
      foreign hands, lies, lies.

Storms in Siam

Streams of silk, soft,
    sent by a slender weaver's hands,
        a fabric gentle as a mouth,
    kissing every leaf and flower,
        licking the stone to jewel.
Then a rough touch,
    a thicker stitch,
        and the sky is calloused.
A net of burlap woven by a giant
        whips down on the world.

Shutters slam all down the street,
    echoing each other.
There is a race of flesh and closing shops.
Abandoned papers dance through pigeon-flight.
The peddlers gather their bracelets and pipes.
Umbrellas in the market blow down.
In their houses, the children stamp
    like anxious ponies.
Secretly, they lean too far out of windows,
    stunned as the cold water
        bites their hands.

Nowhere on earth have I felt it,
this fury of rain, this power.
A river sweeps down the black sky,
    out of God's mouth.
A river floods the world and drowns
        the stars in darkness.
I wash myself in silence,
        watch the lightning pull
        my skin inside out.

Magic, this rain:
       the red dust in the roads
       is a long splash of blood;
       the veins of lightning pulse
       down the sky, always full.

Magic, that the window shattered
           over my bed but did not cut me.
I still have my eyes.
Glass like the teeth of angels
          glitters my skin.

I want to weave my body
       between the cords of rain
       and live in that roar,
          in the giant's mouth,
       dance on his tongue
         on his teeth.

The sky keeps no Yahweh,
       no old white man, white-bearded.
The Devil lives in heaven, howling there.

FOR JUNWEI QI, WHO WENT HOME

In Gansu, in another time,
    your people eat yellow lilies.
The river beyond carries away sand, stone,
        a thousand stories of a million lives.
The landscape of your face
    died before I was born.
Your face is a country even you have forgotten.

The land I come from
    is an old rock with a new skin,
    a world so young that the people
        still smile at sunlight and wind.
Their history breathes lightly,
    quickly, a small animal.

Can you remember the caves
    where you played as a child?
Can you remember the nights
    of shadowed dragons
    and demons on the paths?
Do you still know the colours?

The colour in China, you tell me,
      is often grey.
You say, I know grey as I know
      the inside of my mouth.
You say, Mouths are dangerous places there.
        You marry the first girl you kiss.
        You touch nothing but your sleeves,
          your own naked wrists.
Alone, the skin of your body in the dark
        is a smooth secret.

Junwei, you are gone.
As I write, you return
        to the map on the wall.
You disappear into the intricate fibres
                of the paper,
                into the complex angles
                        of a billion lives,
                                countless fingers and folds
                                        of gleaming hair.

You are lost in Qingyang county
                in the wooden school of a photograph,
                        slightly blurred.
I have not seen China.
That world escapes me.
I do not understand enough.
I become entangled in days
        and lose years
        without reaching the river of your people.

Mandarin sleeps coiled in my skull,
                the snake still twisted to silence,
                        every syllable a cool scale.
I keep the phrases you taught me as prayers.
I remember the tongue is wind-touched,
                the words are danced from the lips.
Think of how I practiced your simple name.

I say it perfectly, still,
                as if I took the word from your mouth and ate it,
                as if I kissed you a thousand times.
Junwei, I can say your name.
That is my offer of love.

NEW LEGENDS: CAMBODIA, 1976
Based on a conversation with Leng J.,
a Cambodian woman living in Thailand

In my country, one legend says
        the stars are not souls
        or the eyes of gods.
It is a new legend
      that makes stars the voices
      of thin women.
We have many stars
        but you cannot hear them.
They are too far away.

The stars are quiet.
They have children
      whose skulls are soft fruit.
They have gentle men who walk
      into the deep green tangle and disappear.

In my country, when you have eaten
      the pet gibbons and the dogs,
        the small crabs
        scuttle in your pockets.
They pinch your tongue
        before you can swallow them.
They are hard and small,
        like the finger bones of children.

The new legends turn rice to maggots.
They coil alive with strange worms,
      with beetles that come
      to clean your sister's feet.
The new legends
are not legends.

They are the only
true stories left.
But no one believes.
No one hears the stars.
Only crickets cry out loud at night.

His ribs are a bird cage.
His heart is a bird,
    a flea-bitten pigeon
    tossing itself against his bones.

The beggars here are ugly poets.
Their rhymes rot in open sores.
They slouch in shadows on boneless legs
    and push tin cups toward my white feet.

Their teeth are black.
They hold their raw hands
    up to me or drag themselves
    like legless dogs.
They know I am neither clean nor honest,
    but lucky.
They know the hole between pity and fear.

If I touched a blind beggar's eyes,
    I might learn his secrets.
If I pressed my pink ear
    to a beggar's mouth,
    I would hear
        that naked bird
        singing above his leather belly,
            each note an answer
            every breath a broken song.

I met you as I met many of your people.

You were selling your wares on the street, poking a note at the *falangs* rushing by: I AM A MUTE ARTIST. Though I stopped, I did not believe you until you opened your mouth. There was no tongue trapped in the gold corral of your teeth.

Twelve blinks later, my face rose from emptiness, a net drawn from blind water. My skin on the paper came from your fingers. This is how you touched me. My friend, you spoke the language of hands. When you wrote, you scribbled Sanskrit like a monk in love with green light through leaves. I did not see the rainbow of clothes and fruit. I did not hear the roar of traffic.

It is possible to laugh without a tongue, and you did. I stayed with you that afternoon, mad white woman, watched you breathe your world into paper, pull lives out of grey lines. Your hands were black with charcoal, gentle and tough as sparrows, light, hollow-boned. You sketched stories to me, dreams, the legends of talking monkeys and flying monsters, half-bird, half-lion. Siamese armies marched over the backs of giants to cross the wild rivers of Burma. You caught the world in the cage of your bronze fingers. You showed me the brilliant walls you made, the murals surging purple and crimson. Your own face came away from an ancient painting, tiger eyes in brown silk. Ten lives ago, you did not live on Sukhumvit.

At night when the streets only smelled of people and
breathed rats, we walked the maze of the city of angels,
through lanes narrow as sleeping eyes. A storm over the city
made you dance; its rain on your skin was the song you
understood perfectly but could not sing.

How much did I pay for that first sketch of my face, the
one I still have tacked to my wall? It is creased, the charcoal
wanders from its first path, the paper is grey now.

I did not pay enough. I cannot. Nothing I have is worth
your hands and their good words. I would give you my own
tongue to hear you speak the language that your fingers
know.

She has lost her way in the streets
    of purple cloth and copper skin.
Wandering alone in the city,
    she finds the veins of silk and gold.
The hilltribe men laugh at her sharp nose, her chalk fingers.
The beggars smile from their caves of tin.

The roads fray to paths scattered with green-eyed goats,
    to old houses splintering now
    and dreaming ghosts.
They lead to temple yards burning rose and orange
    where voices chant inside bells of wind.
The stone shoulders of giants curve to sleep.
Dragons with scales of glass close their tired jaws.

The paths darken to wagon ruts
    deep with the hoof-prints of oxen.
They swirl down to blue-roped rivers
    banked by flowers and mud.
Women there stand in waist-deep water,
    twisting silver from their hair.

She walks to a clearness and looks back at the city's old face.
The green light of the field trembles around her.
She hears frogs and crickets but listens
    to the song of her blood.
For the first time, she understands
    the words.

Glanjanna is an old word for gold.

Jingjoke is the lizard on the wall.

You only knew the storm of song
    that makes this language.
You only glimpsed the fields
    and the fire acrobats for a breath.
You knew me, but only said:
    Karen, you've been here too long.

Your eyes were strange, blue,
    then green eyes blue-grey,
    and so grey this sky
        with Thailand's new rains.
You should have stayed here.
You should have learned
    to stand beneath the spill
        of hot days.
You could have learned the secrets.
But it was not enough for you,
        and too much.
When the scorpion ran across your hand,
        you were more afraid
        than the children.

You took the skin off your heart
    to come here
    but no one wanted it.
The markets are a crimson roar of meat,
        monkey, bull, goat hearts.
Most human hearts end quietly, weak.

If the country is a dream,
     you, asleep in the teak shadows,
          are a dream within a dream.
You will wake from it soon,
     when you rise against the raining sky.

A hand of wind with a hundred fingers
     will smooth the turtle's back
          into pure jade.

The green country will fade
     while you find your fork
     and folded napkin.

The people of the dream will die,
     churn into the old earth,
          disappear.

     I will be among them.

My Skin, The Bitter Colour

I

A hot country, but cold nights
    kill the mornings.
In the back of the truck,
I scrawl out the fields green,
        shadowed grey like the shell
           of a turtle.
I write with hands numbed by wind.

The market women cannot believe
    the paper and serious black ink.
They laugh at me.
One hugs a red-feathered chicken
    to her chest.
We ignore the baskets
    of maize and tobacco.
We ignore the wailing goat.

Who speaks English?
Only one, a man, a teacher
    who leans towards me, grinning.
I cover the words with my hands.
We see through white skin, he says.

II

If we walk together in daylight,
        they weave ropes between us
                with their eyes.
We never speak English
        because they might imagine our words.
If we walk together at night,
        they send the children to follow us.
Always, we feel songs shiver
                down our backs, stones rattle behind us,
                tongues of laughter touch our ears.
I understand the songs now,
                but I cannot have them.
My skin is a bitter colour.

III

Your skin is wood cleaned by rain.
All your bones are blades thrown into muscle.

The gentle people smile over strong teeth.
The bats have eyes and voices for the dark.
The lizards will not keep this secret.

Of all the words, you only tell me
        hum rong-hai na,
        it is forbidden to cry.
I touch your hands,
            not your face, in parting.
Your eyes are painted on temple walls
            and mine are made of ice.
My skin is snow.

My blood is wrong.
It runs backward through my body,
        as clear as a river of salt.

        Chun luk teur.

PART THREE

She Arrives in a
Loose Blue Skirt
Spain

She Arrives in a Loose Blue Skirt
for Nancy Holmes

For all of us, the cynics, the thieves,
     for the penguin-clothed nun shuffling
          patiently in the garden,
     for the mad Gypsy in her rag-coat
          who cries her eyes to the gleam
               of shattered sapphires,
     for each one of us and for no one at all
          but herself

          she has arrived.

We are bitter and small.
Almost all of us have soured hearts,
     little sucked lemons left on the cutting stone.
And we are warped mirrors who lie against each other,
          sharply, sharply, shuddering.
We reflect each other's scars and call this love.
What am I?
I do not merit her arrival.
Has she come for me?

She is already here, saying,
     No, you fool, snuff your poor metaphors,
          don't write it like that. Say,

          hearts like lemons, fresh, brighter
            than the purest gold, and better smelling

          then: we touch all down each other's lengths,
            like mirrors laid together, reflecting light.

She has no use for the muddy comfort of misery.
She has never needed excuses.
If you are bleeding, she chuckles and says,
            How rich the colour is!
            How healthy you are!

Yes, here she is, she has arrived:
            Spring
            has come
            yet again,
         in spite of us.

She is the lovely woman in the loose blue skirt,
      in white lace, dancing clouds
      and southern wind around us.
She turns, spreads her voice of swallows
            and mourning doves over us like a pale sheet.
Her breasts smell like apples,
            her mouth of wine,
            her strong white thighs like fresh bread.
Her wrists are made of roses and her hair
            is softer than dawn-mist.

She has the grace of grass lengthening green,
      effortlessly, grass that sees as cats' eyes see,
               through darkness,
      grass thick and fleshed enough to eat.
I am jealous of the fat horses, the clumsy burros
      clicking their hooves on gravel.
They nuzzle their silk noses in her free salads,
      in her flowers; they chew and chew,
      deeply pleased.

Spring comes, and Spain rolls over on her back,
              belly rabbit-soft.
How ever did this miracle happen?
If you did not live between these sunsets,
        you would not believe they could exist:
                the sun rains flowers, flowers tumble
                    out of heaven's mouth, pale roses,
                    lilacs, violets, orange blossoms.
The dusks are fire:
        yet there you stand, in flame,
            and do not burn.
Just darkness touches you, gently,
        like a warm and lonely body wanting only
            to kiss you to sleep.

Dazed lovers wander up the cliffs
        lazy as kites, arms looped loose around waists,
        over shoulders, eyes brimming ocean
        and hair tangled with sea-wind.
They are, yes, honestly, in love.
They are drowning happily
        in each other's skins,
                pressed closer than barnacles,
                smiling.
See the wet glimmer of their mouths.

You think, My God, I must have dreamt it,
        that people hurt each other,
        it was a nightmare,
        never true.
The lovers have been this gentle
        since the first morning.
Their faces have always been open, plied
                like winded skies,
                like ripe and velvet flowers.

Yes, here she is, and we are still alive
        to see her dance past us in the *paseo,*
        to watch her lean down among us
            like a silver-feathered swan.
The folds of her skirt brush our legs
        as she slips through fences
            and over stone walls,
        flicking awake emerald-eyed lizards,
        tapping the coiled shells of snails.

She has climbed upwards and is singing
        at the top of her lungs from the tops of trees.
Among the invisible clouds of sparrows,
        her voice rises
        and swoops down

        to everyone, especially to the stones
            and small children,
            who hear perfectly.

The frayed stray Gypsy laughs at this music,
        ecstatic, dances a swirl on the beach, strangely
                alone.
But the little rocks and opal shells glisten their own rhymes
        beneath her leather feet, and the anxious choir
                of stars tremble with song.

Her light on the sea slides to us
        in long sheer glitters,
        gold-embroidered cloth
                rolling off the earth's table.
They speak to each other, Spring and the water.
Listen to the sea chanting.
Believe the spring whispering,
                yes, even the smallest words:
                        those curled pink under mossy wood,
                        those nestled in branches,
                        receive the words,
                                the ones folded silver and cool
                                        in the blades of rain,
                                believe those words.
Children and puppies cock their heads to listen,
                and open mouths to swallow the moon.

The ugly Gypsy is beautiful
        as she winds up the *paseo*, drunk,
        head flung back like a door to the sky.
She smells like a wet mongrel, does not know her age,
                cannot read,
                but her hands are wide open.
She is catching all the words of the first showers.
She is catching them with filthy fingers,
                in a rotted comb of teeth,
                in a matted web of hair.

        but her eyes are two jewels, glistening blue,
                worth greeting this rain,
                worth the arrival of the Woman herself.

THE DISORDER OF LOVE

Great love is always the result of a past mistake.

—Tolstoy, from
Anna Karenin

THE ORDER EPHEMEROPTERA

. . . desire perishes
because it tries to be love.

—Jack Gilbert

Riderless

Times ago, I heard your voice
        drifting down the river
        and this journey began.

At night I am coming
towards you, loping
easily over the land.
Sweat chills my face and back.
I will run riderless like this until I find you.

From the last hard tongue of tundra
        to the forests
        where wolves hide in curtains of snow

        I have been searching for you

        past foxes and weasels who swivel
        their chiselled skulls to watch me run.

From the forests to the fields
        where the owls bear down
        like blizzard-winged phantoms
Through the foothills chanting higher and higher,
        watch how the mountains surround me,
        rise at my naked flanks like white-hooded monks
                hungry for the moon.

The moon is a mouth spilling opal
but I don't want her.
Her body is cold and her heart is a bone.
She never bleeds and she cannot sing.

At night I am coming towards you.
When I find you we will not be lost.
It does not matter how far you've wandered.
I will bring you back with me,
show you the sun-drinking fields, the forests,
the rapids where I swam my mad ballets.
The mountains in daylight will be cathedrals
of stone and pine and soprano wind.

There I will lay open the supple earth of my body,
    this hot plain breathing from breast to belly.

I will give you this, my own wild acre of Brazil.

The Innocence of Doors

Across the hall, his guests
     are keeping me awake.
He leaves his doors open, always.
The people laugh hard as whisky melts
     their throats, oils their eyes.
Their whispers are the size of ospreys.

I have heard this before, in another house.
Once I lived near the ocean,
     where the people slept in vaults of gold light
     and woke humming to dance at night, their fingers
          strumming skin.

I told them
     Leave me alone
     Don't sing
     Stop singing!

     Their voices tangled the air.
          They looped me in and gave me a black-eyed centaur.
          I learned to live naked there.

Now I live in a rocky place
     and breathe ice-wind.
My awkward hands cradle stone.
I wear wool.

But the voices across the hall
     are green frogs laughing,
     leaping from one tongue to another.
The man who lives in that room
     makes love to the wind and opens
     his doors to the moon-washed sky.

All day I write.
At night, I want human letters.
I want him to braid his songs into my hair.

But what curious kisses could I whisper in his ear?
My tongue is dipped deep blue in ink.
My hands sink through a quicksand of words.

Close these eyes.
Touch my lips and stretch my body smooth
     in the bed of their naked laughter.
I fall asleep to the sound
     of voices across the hall, opening,
          glowing throats beyond the wall.

How long can we live with these doors so open?

THE LESSER AMAZON

Last night I dreamt
I was the salamander
who does not burn in fire:
I swallowed saffron tongues of flame.

In South America, tree frogs live
in the pooled water of bell-shaped leaves.
They never touch earth but make their choir
in a ripe canopy, serenading higher
than the skulls of hunters.

Those very frogs leap from my rhododendron
into the kitchen sink.
Shreds of jungle dazzle the old house.
Where are all these vines growing from?
This morning a parrot torpedoed over the table.
Yesterday afternoon in the bathtub,
after a surge of curious hissing,
I found a nest of baby snakes beneath
the bathmat, living red leather,
tongues flicking an ancient orange.
They covered my feet in an exotic reptile weave,
wound up my shins, looped themselves
around my waist and neck, slid anxiously
through my slick hair.
It took me an hour to comb them out
and send them slithering to the garden.

It can't go on like this.
The neighbours gossip:
    Has she seduced baboons?
    Is she making love to panthers?
Birds of paradise have chased away the sparrows
and the problem with peacocks
is the potency of their screams.

Creatures peer from the trees
of these turquoise nights, listening
to me rush through the rainforest of my body,
searching for you.

Deep into cardinal soil I plunge my hands,
praying to plant you in this jungle.

Love, my throat is the lesser Amazon.
I want you to slide in.

Carve a slim-ribbed canoe.
Learn how to swim.

THE PURE ANIMAL

Now do you see, now
do you feel them?

Watch the animals waken around us,
inside, see these creatures pant
and pace through their paintings,
anxious to escape the canvas, eager
to prowl the night garden
of this house.

Don't fear them, you're animal yourself,
these heights are ours, these subterranean caves.
Don't be afraid of the depths,
drowning, let your body drop
through this bed, a cream ocean, feel
the undertow of twisted sheets,
the waves of feather and fin.

I throw my limbs up like ropes
to haul you in, the mane of your hair
falls down, wind and scent rise
from your neck like the earth
where you have run.

No metaphor is wet enough,
no metaphor is right,
these words never touch
     the skin and teeth, never feed
     the starving arms, never loosen
     these legs that long to gallop
        down the night.

You rear up like a horse
  (my arms the ropes that rein you in)
   your blood vaults through
    the meadow of your skin

  and just seeing you waken, rise like that,
   just seeing you shudder
    floods me, the inland sea, the inlet
    the in, in, in

When you give me yours, take mine,
fruit cleaves from the stone,
our sinews twist cobra from our bones

The animals around us waken.
The animals in us rise wild.

This is everything, we make this, love,
  this is us, the panther in the museum
   when it springs from the canvas
    in a precise torrent of black and gold,
    crimson paw prints on the polished floor,
    all the doors broken open

The Cheat

The sky unbraids her oyster-blue hair,
hurls rough pearls of hail at my skin.
One man flees over the flesh
of a continent surging in spring.

The other man is here, the man I crush
like the mad one who slams the door shut
on her lover's fingers, who cannot stop
slamming the door, cannot stop.
He cries now in the small room.
He opens a plate glass window with his fist
and walks into the rain.
He will wander this city for hours,
wearing my old coat.

I cannot wear it myself now.
The nerves of his pain still spark
and snap inside it.
Fury clings like a gargoyle
to the shoulders,
the long sleeves,
the rain-whipped back.
The man feeds this gargoyle
like he once fed me, a famished lover.

Once I thought I knew my heart, that red
kestrel soaring in such a shallow sky.
Now I can't see it, I don't know where it is.
I find vultures cleaning their beaks on my ribs.

After sins luxurious, mundane,
count the faces cut with sorrow.

What can I do with so much pain?
There is no suitcase big enough for it,
no abyss deep enough to bury it,
no incinerator for the burning eye and heart.
We tether the shreds of ourselves together
and cry it, cry it, cry it,
until the bed is soaked,
and hemlock sprouts delicate lime
from the sweaty folds of the sheets.
He whispers, *Your body sowed this poison.*

ONE MORE WOMAN BEGS TO
COMPLETE HER LOVER

Once upon a time
they twined tight
round the spool in my gut,
but now the songs unravel in the singing.
Words knot around the table legs,
the arms of chairs, our wrists.
Words spin down to the bed
like maple keys that will never
open the earth.

Oh Joseph.
I've torn a hole in the sky.
Fly through.

Why do you turn away
to watch the small yellow bird
dance and chatter in his kingdom of weeds?
Why do you wring your hands like unclean rags
after steeping them in my hot gloss?

I am an open door.
Walk away after entering but
        step through me.

Come across this threshold—

This Dumb Melodrama

I leave you on the highway beside a cemetery.
Crooked headstone teeth grin and leer.
Farther up, road-kill gives a feast to the ravens.

Christ, to get fed
so simply.
Enough poetry.
I'm sick of it,
        Whitman and the elegies,
        the oatmeal and apples in your pack.
The wind plucks a senseless tune
on your shrouded guitar.

I push you from the borrowed car,
kiss the mouth you've lent me these months.
Hurry, hurry, go now,
cut your poetic tongue
out of my mouth.

I leave you by a field of green wheat.
Grasshoppers razor blind against the wind,
strike your wrists, the book in your hand.

*   *   *

I drove away howling love
in perfect time with wind
thrashing hair in my eyes.
A wasp died skewered on sunlight
against the back window.
You caught a ride east.

I am learning this,
the list of what I do not own.

Least of all, I do not own those roads you travel now,
the steel arteries of this country
pumping petrol blood, the earth's muscles
torn open and and beaten black with asphalt.
I do not own the spring-born mud.
The fierce engines roar on without me.

I untie myself from the tracks
of this dumb melodrama.
Stand up filthy, covered
in dust and pigeon shit,
a fool, a fool.

But I stay here.
I will not follow
fear, your one-eyed
highway, your backward
migration.

THERE ARE CHARMS FOR EVERY
KIND OF JOURNEY

A bird I've never seen threads a desolate song
through this labyrinth of pines.
Dusk comes, then the indigo oil of night.
Mountains dive and rise like dolphins.
Tonight I will dream of the Bay of Biscay,
the shores where I will breathe without you.
You cannot sleep by the sea.

If you were still here, I would whisper,
    Lay your hand on my back.
    This moment is all.
    There will be no more.

Train whistles pierce every black hour,
wise arrows in this witless heart.
The engines cry, Come away come away.

You once said, It's hard to lie in the mountains.
Then you lied beautifully, without blinking.
We are not clean enough to live here.

You left weeks ago,
I leave tomorrow at dawn.
Simplicity is the birthright of deer
who do not name days or plan betrayals.
My life is a broken bridle
and yours is an antique clock.

I wanted to give you a talisman
whose loss wouldn't maim me.
There are charms for every kind of journey.
You needed an owl's black claw,
or a scorpion imprisoned in amber
or my anklebone.

The trains in this deaf country
don't hold people anymore
but I'm going to find one
to drag my heart away from this valley.

I need a train.
I need that kind of weight and roar
to rip your gentle lyrics out of my mouth.

Dear Joseph

Late afternoon, it's raining.
This is the only letter I will not send.
We've axed the noble goodbyes, the relentless jokes.
I must do this, you said, *I regret nothing.*
You suck your vision of wholeness
like a boy sucking a tarnished penny.

You are so rich.

You are not here, old lover.
Someone else already sleeps in sheets
I've not yet washed.
I mourned for a month.
Disgusting, isn't it,
the hip bones gnashing
in that creaky bed.

Even this beautiful house, we've beaten.
Boxes, torn books and letters, crumbling roses
litter the hallway and living room.
Two large moths, soul-mates, have died
and dried in my tea pot.
I rub the powder of their failed flights
between my fingers.

I trip over books on the floor
to find the pen which scribbles this
last note to you, my own true heart

my own true heart because you told me,
     Understand: I do not love well.

I sit in a cream slip, dirty hair uncombed.
If I were willow-boned, Blanche and I
could be sisters, the setting is perfect,
the torn dress in the closet,
the gas stove, the guilty bottle.
But not me, I'm no weeping willow,
my shoulders are too broad,
my accent northern.

Rain crashing there, past my neck, on the window,
as a spider unfolds over the sill, hooking
eight hair-thin limbs over the African violet.
On the stereo, the Russian composer
gifts Scheherezade with a voice again,
sets her pirouetting from one stunning story to another.

The king begins to adore her mouth,
the way she licks her lips, inhales so quickly ...
He sees her splendid teeth are ivory and knows
he can never kill her, she must live on
with him, he loves her silken see-through words.

But this is hardly Arabia
and I was never a virgin princess.
My clothes are wrinkled and practical.

My underwear dry out their loneliness
in the bathroom.

I let the plants die.

Autumn comes early.

Who loves well?

Temporarily

The details of your face escape like minnows.
                                        —Don McKay

I abandon men,
temporarily,
and come to the cabin.
I sit on the porch mending
the messy tear in my left ventricle.
Night blues the lake,
sweeps the shore with raven-wing.
A moth beats an ash tattoo
against the lampshade.

Inside, the women play cards, drink,
and laugh with occasional hysteria.

I've spent a third of my life
listening to those sounds,
envisioning pillows, pliable
hand-warmed cards, assorted glasses.
I've learned to drink Scotch and beer,
negotiating entrance to those pools of talk.

It does not matter.
Human waters drain away from me.
The women in the other room howl.
They discuss an older woman's ugly hair.

Has anything on earth ever been so funny?

Morning, I walk into the orchard
of apricot sky, crushing Venus's slippers
and shooting stars with glee.
I stop at the locoweed
like a starving cow and
eat, eat.
Later I slide the canoe out,
inhale the wide death of rivers.
I consider drowning.

Unfortunately, I am a strong swimmer,
it would take an alligator
or an Atlantic storm to haul me under.

Hours later, when I glide
fierce and burnt along the dock,
the expensive puppy barks,
shakes light from its pedigree fur.
The mistress of canoe and cabin
turns over on her towelly spit.
She yawns, extraordinarily
bored with her magazine, and asks

Did you have a nice time?
Isn't the lake lovely?
Aren't you afraid of the depth
out there?

* * *

I sit in the shade for so long
my feet grow cold, though the heat
of high summer is a royal iguana, languid,
lording over the stones near the lake.

I no longer wait for Joseph.
On a phone his dead voice intoned,
Do not think of me as your lover

and I do not, I watch birds devouring moths instead
(vowing: I am no dull moth)

No, I do not think of him.
I disremember him.
I summon his naked reflection out of my mirror.

He is not my lover, I sing to myself, plucking
his finger-husks from the spiderweb above my bed.
I bait fish hooks with my own bitter grubs
and eat rainbow trout until my eyes feel blue.

I swim miles above star-rippled rocks.
No one knows, but the whole lake
is laden with opals and moonstones.
I walk alone on the dirt roads.
Trees lean over to touch my shoulders
like the lover I no longer have.

Oh, to sleep in those jade palaces of shade,
those alcazars of leaf and shadow.
Earth's emerald scent thrives inside me.
When I howl in a blown sea of wheat,
no one can tell my voice from the wind's.

* * *

The inhabitants of my life:

birds whose names I learn and forget

these flowers lying on the table
like faeries fast asleep

the disgruntled porcupine bristling under the moon,
snorting at me when I come out with a candle

that woman down there in the water, smiling,
talking philosophy, fashion, gin rummy.
She bobs on a styrofoam cloud.
Her hair unlike the ugly hair of old women,
she floats, with elegance, towards death.

* * *

And the child, I cannot forget
the neighbour's child,
whose eyes are scattered with fresh hay.
Sunset writes the lyrics of a girl's limbs
in blue water, her body
sheathed in green as she dives,
hands hungry for the pulse of stone.
Above her, long gold spoons stir the lake.

Pulling herself up on the dock,
she is the mermaid fool who surrendered her tail.
Her skin shivers beneath
the velvet curiosity of bees
who believe her dress is a garden.
Lacewings halo her knees,
copper threads shine in her drying hair.

I kiss her cool forehead.
She dances on the dock.

EPHEMEROPTERA

In the beginning, I was young, I whispered:
    your words fill my body's well
    your voice ripens stone
    your words run the river emerald.
In the beginning I was very young.

We went to a lake.
The great pelicans flew
slowly, like exhausted angels.
At night the torrent of your fingers
made me pant
    Believe in this Believe in this
though it was a lie.

Yes. Our bodies lied.
Your weight crashing down
like earth from a mountainside
had nothing to do with the truth.
A natural disaster, yes, but what
was I doing in the mountains anyway?

I scraped my ankle on the rocks
watching the most vivid rainbow
we had ever seen
but that, too, was a false sign.
I wish the cut had been deep enough
to leave a scar, I wanted
something to remember you by.

Nothing was true enough to stay.
Now I drag a stick through the gutter
of my memory, searching for leftovers.

The mayflies.
Miniature dragons fluttered around us
those days by the lake, clung
to the cabin screens, landed in our hair.
The order *ephemeroptera*.

Born without true mouths, they rise from the water
only to mate, even food unnecessary
when clean biological lust is life.
Our naked feet crushed thousands on the roads.
Cheap tar and the seasonal carnage of mayflies
designed our soles, stuck to our heels.

Now lean over, Joseph, look into the well.
Not your exquisite voice ringing there
but dead insects blinding the water's eye.

The vision of Mary turning
    in a crowded room, wordless,
        to embrace me.
        She was too slender, shoulders roped
          to her neck with green ribbon.
        Her husband sat on the edge of a chair,
          eyes like gouged clay,
          whispering, *I love her.*

Do not dream of these people anymore.
Like the dead, they inhabit severed countries.
They wake and sleep at different hours.
As you envision them, they might live
those exact movements
with other people,
but never with you.

You twist awake in a cold room
with too many windows.
Scarves and sheets curtain out the street.
Someone has given you irises.
Littered paper on the floor demands attention.
Shaquil has left a note saying he is broke,
will you lend him money?
In the narrow bed, a book suffocates
under your elbow.

Pour the people of the dream into a kettle,
boil them.
They evaporate.
Do they settle on your ceiling?
Or do you drink them with your coffee?

Because night after night, they rise
    from you anew, explaining themselves,
        furious, and he makes love to you again,
            and again she cries,
                and Gabriel cuts up
                    photographs and old snakeskins
                    and a dozen books.

The dreams are untrue, too beautiful—
    the black-haired man sings a path
        through mountains now,
    once more you tear
        a cotton dress over your head
        and find your body clean beneath it.

You rise angry in the dark,
rummage for the knife Jacques gave you.
Twice this new knife has almost
relieved you of your thumb.
You slice away the visions without blinking,
heave them to the cats in the vacant lot,
who are always hungry.

But you lie awake, suspended
in a hammock of shadow and streetlight,
remembering.
Full night long, you listen to the cats
fight and fuck in the skeleton of love,
re-sounding your cries.

You are still listening
when dawn rises from the ground
like a soldier, grey and cold,
afraid of his own power.

The truth is, you were always planning to leave.

The world threw herself open like a laughing woman, like a door made of feathers, like a body of water falling down a thousand fathoms: even the slums of Lisboa and Istanbul heaved like rich oceans. Who could resist such labyrinths, the roads, the street signs with dancing alphabets? The atlas in the study unbound and became an eagle with a snake's tail. It caught you up in its hooked beak.

Now, an ocean distant and a sea away, a sheik from Algeria slaughters a lamb in his bathtub. He cooks the best couscous on the European continent. Over mint tea, he swears you have desert eyes. He wants to take you to Africa, his own oasis, he eases your eyelids down with his brown fingers and describes the blue room of echoing walls where you will sleep . . .

At night, creeks flood your dreams. Paths appear at the edge of the city, trails you know as well as the mare knows them, navigating forever with the star of home on her flanks, between her ears. Half-children curl at the bottom of the pond, lingering in their muddy shells. There are dreams, too, of the man who overthrew you, how you heaved the world upside down to remain standing. God will reward him with warm rooms and diapers. His snapdragons will bloom in December.

The atlas, open, takes you. Who can anchor a heart that longs to be a fish? Thunder, tearing the sheet of sky, takes you. Come, enter this ocean of sharks and shattered light, drink salt and honey by the mouthful. Pay with peace if you have to, but swallow the storm and carry it in your flesh. Why are you afraid to nourish this extravagant desire to devour the world?

Years from now, in a cave in Spain, you will ask a witch if it's greed or a healthy appetite. She will laugh; even her burnished eyes will make a sound like bells. She'll take your face in her hands and whisper, "But, daughter, the world devours you."

The Drowning Stroke

Cities beyond, an abacus
of hours and years reckoned away,
we meet each other again one night

very late, so late.

The whisky and wine alter nothing.
Gold and blood torn from the fruit.
We twist our mouths around small words, quiet
syllables of delight and lost mittens, anecdotes
from New York, phrases from our little towns,
heavy sentences to prove and defend
our present happiness.

You tell me you swam naked
through last summer, you paint
such a clean watercolour,
your wedding ring unsalvageable,
lost among sand dollars and seaweed.

I remember when you could not drink
enough of me.

Remember?
You came with me to watch
the slow gorgeous sharks,
their fins slicing the waves
beyond the breakwater.
You came with me.
You admired their immaculate hunger.
Remember?
I showed you
the throb of animals
in the foam, the tide pool.

Recall the rare anemone
pink and blood-pulsed and opening,
flowering for you.

Remember that.
Forget it now
in the next breath,
in the drowning stroke
of another year.

I smell rot in your hair, Love.
Time's scarring pulls white bars
down my body.
I turn and pace and pivot in my prison
of bone and laughter, a felon
in this flesh you ate
and ate and ate

and fled.

So late, so late.
Can you hear the goblin-ice
gnawing the eyes of the statues?
The ghosts of fish swim black
through the wind on this dying shore.

Don't you know the fishermen here are starving?
Watch their boats list grey and rotten,
bodies swollen with emptiness.
Now do you see them?

Even the vast rocks of this coast
are broken, bones of a giant
who staggered beneath
the frozen weight of stars.

Can't you see them?

And heaving away from the land
we inhabit, as though in fear,
yet still swelling around us
and in our hearts,

behold the squandered sea.

The Disorder of Love

This Woman

Dawn, a bowl of peach light
on the black table of spruce.
The sky yawns into its blueness.
Poplars rub their naked wrists together.
Silence from the earth, enormous and graceful
    as the swooping owl she watched last night.

Like Rembrandt's people breathing out of canvas,
    the horses walk alive from the wakening field,
    push against their frames, the fences.
They stretch out their sleek necks for her.
Even the ugly ones are perfect
    in themselves, strong-backed
    and holy, seraphs whose wings
    have fallen into the water troughs
    and turned into emerald algae.
Jealous ponies chase each other away from her.
Each animal turns slick with spring
as Orion glides under the earth.

Jake steps back into the house and drinks her coffee.
She fills twenty cigarette tubes with tobacco.
The Great Dane groans like a fledgling dragon
and rests his huge head in her lap.
Since her sixth year, she has dreamed
of this belly of peace.
At dawn and dusk she finds it,
in silence and the language of animals.

Her other hours snarl in the city,
in the bowels of a police-station:
    the beaten child wandering the streets of Bowness
    the woman freshly raped, unable to spell her name
    the woman whose husband has locked her in the garage
    the man who finds his son hanging from the rafters

She is intimate with these disasters,
takes the calls with steady hands,
taps in the reports tearlessly.
She declares herself a professional
in the management of human cruelty.
My heart, she says, my poor heart
bangs its head against the walls of the world.

And she coughs her own fairytales, this woman.
Even now, the granddaughter tears up
the city's cliffsides, body scarred
with tire treads and doused in rain.

It's a wet season, she says,
knowing the girl wears sneakers without socks.

In the detention centres, Jake explains,
    the girls play a wicked game.
        They scratch each other until they bleed.
            The winner is the one who does not cry out.
Her granddaughter's arms and hands are striped
        with long scabs of endurance.

Jake, my mother,
at the eternal kitchen table of her life,
her love for her children a symphony, a masterpiece
I haven't the guts to fathom yet.

I watch her face alter under the exacting thumbs of time,
that voracious sculptor who molds us into our dying.
The lines around her eyes are nets
heavy with those nights
drowning in the kitchen,
ashes splashed around her hands,
rye and coke by her forearm,
the cigarette sending up relentless signals.
She watched her own mother beaten,
scalp torn and hair matted with blood.

Now she wakes at 5 am,
puts the tobacco away,
and returns to the porch

where morning appears like one more child
sprawled in the grass,
laughing gold in tiger lilies and peonies.

She stands there smiling, this woman

and says, The sweet peas are coming up.
        The garden's going to sing this year.

STRAY CAT

I know what you saw:
    dawn, the long tawn spill of deer
    through aspen
    the pond a well of clouds
    a dragonfly prying new wings from its old self,
    finished with a childhood of water

I heard what you heard,
filtered through my own flesh:
    the carousing heart
    like a drumming grouse
    or a hammer
    or a fist-beat
        on the guitar's hollow body

See how each thing holds onto the next?
That was the wisdom we were meant to learn
in the woods where we worked and fought
and sucked each other's jealous blood.

Instead we indulged in melodrama and beer,
coyote nights yelping lust,
the music too beautiful for us.
Our backs bowed cold under the stars but our
faces and knees, breasts and feet grew hot
at the firepit.
The flames mocked us for lacking
the courage to burn,
to acquire a taste for ashes.

Funny we called you Cat
when you were the only innocent
bumbling among hard-mouthed women.
Of course I adored you.
Your scent of lemon and berry
turned the cook house tropical.
We drenched ourselves with insect repellent;
you wore perfume.

I remember your blackened eyes,
despair barely concealed under thin clothes,
those limbs determined to provoke desire
in anyone after Nicolas
picked your breastbone clean
and tossed you away.

But most days, your body forgot
its lithe contours, its woman-spice
and arch and slide.
I am not a great beauty, you said
one afternoon, sighing, but that night
I lay awake wondering why on earth
I hadn't argued with you.

You moved among us for free.
Like a child, you gave away your treasures
in exchange for anything
that sang or smelled or stung like love.

I took nothing from you
and I gave you nothing but
the occasional gin and tonic,
red wine in a jam jar,
those black olives and
tomatoes on the porch.

But I adored you,
your tigress appetite,
your willow waist.
I could lift you up
        just like that, into wind after rain,
        into my arms, like lifting the muscled
                slimness of a cat

        the stray you finally notice one evening
                and reach for.
        You look full into her eyes
                and see the flame enslaved,
                        the starving spark inside.

THE QUICK OF HISTORY

We lie on the Abruzzi carpet.
Little else in the living
room except for the desk,
red and blue rice paper prints,
Picasso's dear madman Sebastian,

and paper, scattered
      paper piled
            unsheathed hundreds
                of thin knives

Outside it is snowing.
Every time I live here
it is snowing.
My only life in this city,
the slowest avalanche on earth.

It was my terror as a child
to drown, not in water
but in snow.
They said you didn't know which way was up
or down, you would dig slowly for hours
in the wrong direction, a stupid worm,
freezing to death, crazy
with cold, but you would never
get out, never
escape the heavy white
darkness pressing down, suffocating you
filling your nose eyes mouth ears
all the senses frozen out
gone
      you were trapped
      and no one ever knew.

No one ever knew.

It has been snowing for a long time.

Yet I know I am safe
lying here with you.
One eye brown, one eye blue,
my guileless sorcerer.
Your beard's turning goat-white.
My calloused feet are crossed on your chest.

You pull me closer, taking my hand
to press it down on your torso,
below the ribcage.
        Feel that? you ask, rubbing
my fingers on the hard cords
of gristle under your flesh.
        That's one of the things
        they did to me. Tore open
        the lining of my stomach.

I read the weird Braille of hurt in you,
that scar beneath the skin.
If scars were always visible,
we would be hideous.
Sometimes we're ugly anyway.
Wounds reveal themselves in our voices,
in the way our hands shrink tight
around our assets, in the way
we punish whatever we can.
I know a man who bought a punching bag
and a bible to keep from murdering his father.

The fuckers! you whisper, loudly,
and I howl, Yeah, the fuckers!
Crude agreement is not poetry
but the truth of it is.
Our voices so bare in the bare room.
I am shaking.
We hug each other like two wrestlers
who've suddenly, obscenely, fallen in love.

In this room illumined by winter,
the keen unsentimental light of snow,
we strip history down
until we come to the quick

our raw naked selves
        two children

Then there is only surprise,
a momentary breathless shock:
      we are beautiful.

I'm a cat born in the age of calamity and famine, and I'm looking for you. I know I won't find you.

This city is small but not that small. Funny, to be compelled by idiot hunger. Bloody hilarious, the way lust drags me out of the house by the hair, sends me stumbling down the stairs, keys jingling in my hand like jewels stolen from a drunk, like the bell you wore on your ankle that time, like your bracelets' jangle when you yank the sweater up your narrow back, over your head.

Your face, the sly way your eyes enter mine, then swim away, your hands—masters of puppet jaws and foot massage—your skin, your exploding laughter, who could resist any of it? Or the way you smile as your little brown knife glides under the ripe skin of the mango. "This fruit," you say, "begs to be eaten."

It is difficult to breathe around you. It is difficult to speak any comprehensible language.

You push a thick slice of sweet honey-orange into your mouth, your narrow fingers dripping juice, wet flesh. You gulp some, you chew more, you say, "There are mango trees in the yard of the house where I was born."

Am I surprised? Tropical weather precedes you. Petals of bougainvillaea and jasmine fall after you like pieces of lingerie.

Useless to praise this street, the neon emptiness, this bus-stop bench and traffic snorting toward downtown. Useless. When was the last time I prowled like this, wishing I could rip down a rag of the blue night sky and ravage it whole?

The bus stops, the door swings open.

"Sorry, I'm just writing poetry."

The driver smiles. "That's all right." He pulls the door shut with a wink and drives off, trailing exhaust.

Oh, the exhaustion of confused lust. To hang upside down from the chandelier of desire for a woman who always leaves the party before I do. Who cannot give me her phone number because she has no phone. Who cannot give me her mouth because it is constantly occupied by laughter and slender white cigarettes. I want to eat your cigarettes, Jazz, have I told you? And I don't even smoke.

There's no way to reach you, no way to stretch my hand into your sunlit mornings warm as oranges on the tree. My ass is cold as December marble. You are somewhere in this city but you are not here.

I'm writing this at a bus stop in front of a car-lot on 1st Street. Isn't that pathetic? I'm no longer eighteen, you know, I can't wait until 2 am, I simply won't wait until you walk by . . .

My feet turn into the cement beneath my shoes. I'm finally feeling tired, writing this, I realize you will not materialize bodily out of one of the brand new Volvos behind me.

You've probably moved anyway, maybe you live on 2nd Street, not 1st, maybe you're in love, maybe you never considered the possibilities beyond foot massage, the skin that extends above the bones of my toes, the soft places past the softness in the centre of the foot, an array of nerves like guitar strings in need of tuning, in need of changing.

Cars, the modern pestilence, bellow and roar by the bus stop, a man behind every wheel, men with moustaches, men without, some chiselled Apollos, some in beer shirts and baseball caps. The cylinders in their engines bore me to death.

Finally it's so late and cold I can't write anymore. I am sober and disappointed. My hands are ice-knuckled while somewhere your body is roasted nutmeg. You smoke a cigarette with your Trinidad hands, your tropical mouth. You sip a transparent drink and smile, contemplating all the people who own phones in this world, all the women and men who care who calls.

You lean your head back, your mouth turns loose its laughter like a red colt. Hair falls away from your neck like a mane, like a night waterfall dropping silver, like a veil falling down.

I can see the naked wood of your brown neck.

Wherever you are tonight, I kiss you there.

BURIED AT SEA

I have small hands, especially for a sculptor.
Very small hands. How can they hold the earth?
                                    —Alexandra Keim

Chocolate almonds on two tongues,
grass beneath four elbows.
Love rises in us like the sap
in these tall spruce.

You have a letter from London.
I have poetry from the coast.
Last night your father quoted Pablo
as we sat in the garden:
        Puedo escribir los versos más tristes esta noche ...
        Es tan corto el amor, y es tan largo el olvido

But this morning we eat almonds and tell
each other: the gods exist, remember all.
Holiness is here, poetry on the rug,
a dozen books under the lilacs,
marble and glass breathing,
waiting for you in England.

We lounge in our underwear
reading, arguing about mathematics,
the terrifying equations
of distance and love.
When wind heaves the high trees
around us, they sing
about deep water.

I want to be buried at sea,
you tell me.

It's a very complicated procedure.
You have to start years
before the day you die,
make arrangements for the cage of mesh,
metal, or plastic, as you prefer.
They bury you in a cage
so your limbs don't float
up to the surface,
so you don't frighten the fishermen from Peru
or ruin a young couple's honeymoon cruise.

Who wants to see an errant skull
bobbing in the moonlight,
the smile flashing fishes,
eye-sockets a dazzle of anenomes?
Who wants to meet a ragged leg
sauntering through the waves?

You want to be buried at sea.
I want to live there.
Yet we have nothing
but this morning
alive on the land.
Our bodies have become mysterious
territory for the ants,
who do not comprehend such polished acres.

Bury me at sea, you say
and I laugh.
Surely you know your limbs
already float through the world.
Over the mongrel back of this country,
southward, to El Palacio de los Corazones

eastward, through breakers, to England,
where the silver dragon's tail
roared from your fingers

northward, to St. Petersburg where you wove
a wing for a Russian angel

westward, to Gotland, where the Swedish stones
tell riddles of ancient snails,
wolves' teeth biting the tide,
fish plunging through cliffs.

Already, you are buried in water,
you are buried in earth,
even as you rise above me, laughing.

No cage could imprison those hands.

Believe it:
Already your limbs inhabit
the lands, swim the infinite seas.

TARIQ IN THE HOUSE OF
NIGHT BLUES AND TOUCH

I.

Late nights alone in rooms with a ghost,
the blue-eyed woman who dreamed Italy.
The canary in the window box blazes
shreds of fear.
His name is Caruso,
sad fate.
He never sings.

This, a gilded cage of artifacts,
Afghani carpets and tea pots, old photographs
of people I do not know—
yet how their dead eyes arrest me.

Their eyes vault through a century
and land, without a sound, in my throat.

II.

The ghost of this English house
was born in China.
You were born in Pakistan.
I was born down the street.
Yet we meet here, between the faces
of gracious paintings, our hands around
glasses of gin.
We feel the ice on our hot palms.
We smile.

Yours, the teeth of a king.
Your fingers jointed at the ends
like a Balinese dancer's,
though you explain you are a musician.
We will work together this summer.
You will teach me something about music.

III.

Hands are strange animals,
shape-shifters.
This year my hands are tough, solitary spiders.
My shoulders shrug into and out of sweaters
carelessly, I drink the river
with my own throat, alone.
Silence is its own music
in a house like this,
where symphonies and string quartets
were poured with the foundation,
hammered into the walls, planted with the roses.
Puccini and Verdi compose in each room.

I would like to have commerce with this house
every day, stay inside and breathe
her history as you breathe
a lover's sleep, collecting the eyelids'
tremor like gold dust.

But my days have been bought
by the Alberta government.
I have sold my days: I am damned.
The office slumps like a warty monster
in the foreground of this poem.

Squint. You will see it. It looms
all around you.

iv.

8:15 a.m.
I've already been driving for an hour.
I'm at work behind a metal desk, actively
slaughtering my children.
I crush ten thousand words
like delicate eggs under my own thumbs.
My shape-shifting hands are mallets now,
my hands are murderous bricks.

Friends ask why I sound so foreign
here, in the country of my birth.

When the paycheque witch approaches,
        bearing apples and ribbons,
        combs for my hair,
                poetry squawks away in terror.
Poetry is a bird of paradise
wise to poachers.

If you give your life,
they'll give you a dishwasher,
a Rabbit, a suburban graveyard
to bury it in.

They'll give you all this, and more,
much more, and you will applaud as you watch them
pull the fingers off your soul.
Later, you will experience relief, calm.
Like having a lobotomy but tidier.
No sponges, no scalpels, no visible scars.

v.

You say that if you had lived in Pakistan,
you would not be a musician.
But I think you're wrong.
Even now, the twin you never met is there,
pivoting in the street's river,
its women and men themselves a strain of music.
Your brother stands on the bank of a million lives
in a road splashed with rain and dogs,
the bronze curtain of his body open.

These echoes are inescapable.
These echoes make us
as living sound makes them.
I know this from the old house,
the blue-eyed ghost.

VI.

So much for Greek islands
and swimming naked over
obsidian sand.
It rains every day in July.
The only sunlight in this jungle
filters through your mouth.
All the women's magazines say

DON'T GET INVOLVED WITH A CO-WORKER

so I do it, quickly, quickly as possible.
At least you're not married.
The progress of age.

Still, I understand the great love affair
this summer is between you
and your new guitar.

Look at those curves, you say,
the ideal woman, café-au-lait body,
cello-heart, hooves of Arabian rhythm.

Now, night blues and touch

fingers curved around the pale neck
of the guitar in your arms

Caruso,
the terrified canary,
did not sing
until you came,
played here.

VII.

Slowly. Slowly.
See the vines crave
the broken wall.
Up, up. Down, deeper
through the crevice,
over the edge, into
the garden.

Goldfish light darts in, out of your mouth.
Red leaves grow and fall down the paintings.
An English house, but you bring me to India
beneath the shawl of your body.

Shadows tiger-stripe the table,
the chairs, the walls, the bed.
Your shadow yet another ghost,
such rich black smoke, the cardamom
crushed in the mortar and pestle
of our hip bones and hollows, the cilantro
green on our lips, sandalwood sweat
down the neck.

We oil the cinnamon,
set it aflame like a candle
to cast light,
to ignite
our selves.

The Body Suddenly

The body suddenly
exotic, slick, rising from the desert
like a creature we've never seen before,
    a beast we could not have borne,

        not us, with our hearts dipped in tar,
        tossed on the rocks.

Fledglings born in a parched country,
we licked the salt that ices life,
licked and sucked, insatiable for spoil.

The caves we lived in smelled
of old blood, bitten tongues.
We kept our treasures buried under
a blanket of sand and lies.
I did not know you then
but at night I prayed
for an animal like myself,
any woman who coveted silver
and sunlight, the ruthless glint
of the real.

Common guilt gifted us with each other.
Ours the sin of shining in a grey country.

* * *

Your body suddenly
broken into light, pried open
in the dark, a pomegranate
of blood and flower.

I dip my hands into the river
of you, the long sweet waters
of your body

and the desert draws back,

the desert dies.

TOMORROW YOU WILL BE IN AFRICA

For Sandra and David
talisman and prayer,
a poem for your journey

Black dogs barking in the snow.
Midnight in the back alley, white
holding down every sound
just a moment longer.
The candleflame is not high enough tonight.

Tomorrow you will be in Africa,
and I am crying.

                  * * *

With you gone,
what can I love?

                  * * *

With you gone,
how will I laugh?

How will I escape the beast
that stalks the city, the giant
shopping mall we all fear?
Franchise food slides into franchised bodies.
Ah, the grease of complicity!

Construction sites in the piggish suburbs:
the fresh-dug basements are very large
open-mouthed graves, big enough
for entire dysfunctional families,
fully-equipped rec rooms, two metre television screens,
personal computers, hundreds of plastic
and nylon sex toys.

                    *   *   *

You are a raging bull
with two Leicas around your neck.
All the idiot world's wearing red.
Fury aside, your laughter is God's own
personal joke, contagious,
a holy plague.

And you are the delicate
twelve-year-old with blue lights
in your face; eyes that shine open
the shuttered world.

Always between us, beneath us,
words, words like a raft
of half-rotted timbers.

Listen, you told me,
trying to convince yourself,

          This raft will be enough
                  we will learn to navigate by the stars
                  we will study the winds
                  we will remember the ways of salt and blood
          This raft will take us home.

* * *

Oh, Africa.
I am too small.
How can I know your greatness?

They have promised me your paper-thorns
and a tiger's eye.
They will send faces from the land,
a deep poem about your sky,
an envelope coated, inside,
with sienna dust.

Africa,
from this winter,
with all my ignorance,
I ask you:

    Please, take care of them.

PANDORA STREET, LATE NOVEMBER

When I woke up
it was raining
and she was gone.
The window was opened
to the silver
eyes of the world.
My shoulders were cold.

The sound of horses' hooves
clapping the road outside
made me think
I was in another country

but I wasn't.
I was in this country,
land of my body,
naked and alone.
I heard rain falling
off the roof.
I could not hear
the ocean.

On the desk
the driftwood we had gathered
the day before, two mottled stones
like petrified eggs,

and her note, written on hotel stationery,
a short treatise on the inadequacy
of my hands, the failure
of vagabond lust

(each word self-conscious,
innocently vengeful,
each word aware
it was not a wave,
not a wind,
not her warm mouth):

       You still don't know
       anything
       about me.

ALEXANDRA

She lay upstairs
inhaling the night,
asleep, her hair unbound on the pillows.
Mouth open slightly, her face
grave and beautiful, engaged
in the fervent waltz of sleep.
Both arms flung open over the burgundy quilt.
She was dancing motionless like that
when I left her
and came down in the dark
to watch the moon, white,
rove over the whiter hills.
I thought of nothing but
her breasts,
my mouth.

I sat crying in front
of the big window, filled
with the inchoate emptiness
of moon-sky and snow.
I was feeling the surprise of it,
the absurdity, even,
and the absolute rightness
of such a landscape.
The way her ivory back was
like my own but smaller,
a smooth plain of
heat, strength, the long
hunger that leads
to the mouth,
to the cunt.

I had never seen so much
clean white turned platinum,
rose-purple, blue in the dark.

I sat in the silent house.
For awhile, coyotes.
Once, her cough,
which made me still and hopeful
because it had the raw silk
of her voice in it.
I wanted her to call my name,
but she slept on
turning slowly in her dance,
tangled in tassels of dream
and breath, quiet

because I had loved her
well enough.

She has no idea
how awake I am,
after such long sleep:
it doesn't matter.
This is the way things
are now, these hills,
my life filled with
depths, roundnesses,
the deep basins of the land
she lives in,
the land she is.

MONTREAL

We are back again in winter.
As lovers we leave behind the blankets
    and face the real mirror,
        the glimmering imprisonment of hands, our faces,
          all the world's nakedness
            in these two bodies.

Two mornings in Montreal.
Even this ashen light reveals too much.
Another day in another apartment.
A bed on the floor.
Someone else's sheets
    and then the difficult mystery of
      who has slept here and
        what colour was her hair

One wine-coloured earring
on the piano

water glass, old water

another dirty window pane
    avalanche of concrete outside
      a small man floundering in the snow
        the alley like a frozen tongue

(though even now, we know,
a building burns in this city,
black icicles hang from
flame-shattered windows)

What I have loved always
    is the way your body insists
        on summer, the drum
            pounding *inside* your fingers.

What I have loved always
    are your hands, your
        voice the source
            of summer, those hours,
                tons of light firing
                    the mountain rivers.

Tons of snow flood
    the streets of Montreal.
Another radiator
    inhabited by nails
        and water snakes.
Another telephone ringing,
    ringing, a voice from
        a separate star singing
            your name.

This has nothing to do
    with betrayal
        and everything to do
            with different time zones

I break my neck
    tripping over clouds
        and continents.
You sit naked
    at the out-of-tune piano
        playing anyway.

You are a map gently torn
    with folding and refolding.
I am chaos in a dress, dragging
    a suitcase of wind and shells.

What I have loved always
    are your hands
            that hold the birds of summer
    and let them go
    let them go all at once

        singing

EVIDENCE OF GOD

The colour of Canadian rye whisky
is not really the colour of amber
or liquid gold
but more the colour of my mother's voice
when she is drunk,
too warm, embarrassing,
an out-of-tune guitar played in minors
so you know the player is dishonest,
not to be trusted, dangerous
as only the deeply sentimental can be,
because they dread
the sandpaper hands
of the truth.

Not to say my mother is dangerous
but of course she is, we all are
when we hurt those who love us
when our own pain overshadows
the blessings and reminds us
of nothing but our pain,
our own pain, our own pain.
It's a boring litany, but popular,
difficult to unlearn, difficult
to forget, as the lines to bad songs
always are.

I can't blame her really,
but sometimes I do.
It wasn't so bad anyway,
though it was, and the badness
lives on and on, I can't kill it.
It's like one of those deathless Chinese demons
I've been reading about.
All demons are deathless,
unlike sisters and brothers.
Demons are the colour
of Canadian rye whisky
and weeping, the colour of
the turquoise scarf
my brother stole years ago
and sold.

He is selling again, not scarves,
drugs, though I believed for a time
he was home, in his senses.
When we talk now, it is once again
through fog, the ungraspable cape of a demon.
When he speaks I cannot hear
his voice, I hear the little asshole
gargoyle gnawing his heart.
My brother doesn't understand.
He opened his mouth and begged the demon in.

Of the body, I love the hands most,
but I see my family is a family of mouths,
of openings and closings, ingestations,
vomit, grunts, and howls.
Hands naked remind me of tree branches,
mouths remind me of graves, isn't that strange?

But that's what I see, my brother
breathing demons, my mother
drinking them, my father owned
by them now, hung in their barren realm
like a scarecrow on a stake, still blinking.
My sister ate demons and ate them
and finally choked to death on their bones.

I, too, am a creature of the mouth, the tongue.
But I am a lucky one, I learned the difficult
and late-night art of singing demons
out of me, out of my body, away
into the wind
or onto paper

where they are
no longer demons

but gifts.

CHAOS IS A GREEK WORD

walk here girl
where everything
answers your nakedness

—Kenneth White

FRAGMENTS

What fills a day?
Grace and poison,
the body of a snake.

The almond shell
cradles the tree.

Dusk, when dust comes
gold and certain stones
the colour of his hands,
full of blood, signed
by scars.

Only the white horse
is saved from the black
swallow falling, night.

Candle in the dark.
Come the moth, the praying
mantis with agile hands.
How she plucks the red beetles,
like rosebuds, from the breeze.

Splendid minnows, the meteors,
shoot from deep space
into the shallows of the sea.

A man walks away.
In his arms he carries
thick swathes of oregano.
A hundred bees follow him
singing like children.

When he whistles
absentmindedly
a naked woman wakes
in a stone house.

At dawn, a red scorpion walks
slowly across her notebook.
The best Greek lesson.

Goat's horn,
truth that grows like stone.
Spun-gold eyes.
The white flame of milk.

Bent back, a drum beaten by sunlight.
Every rib a xylophone key.
The world plays me.
A breeze in the windpipe,
wind held by the silver fingers
of the olive trees.

Every garden bends the knees.
The men of this island pray
long hours in the sun.

Promise you will return.
Return and touch
the sea-tamed stones.
Return and stand here
with naked feet.

Offer your face
to the water.
Offer your one life
to this last blue
altar of sky.

Yiorgos and Shipake

Kitten-surge out of the wooden wheelbarrow,
green and scarlet garden-splash up the fence.
Yiorgos rides in, horse caravan
jingling bells, saddle-tools, trunks
bulging leather, silver-spilling pouches.
Wilderness of white hair overruns his head.
He plants a garden across the road,
hangs a bed in the biggest olive tree.
I meet him at the water-tap in the road.
I have curiosity for you, he says.

Mornings we slurp thick coffee,
see distant ships drop off the horizon.
I watch him dance with his horses.

* * *

This spring the bay colt
sheds his coltishness and bucks
at the touch of a saddle.
He spends hours whetting his hooves
on the stony cliffs above the sea.
Finally, wind charging towards afternoon,
he breaks from the mare
with his first real scream,
a savage toss of mane and muscle.

Tethered, the mare tries calling him back,
but he gallops hard for the gate, through it
and down, pounding the hillside, towards Maria
and her terrified sheep.
He's weaned himself, Yiorgos laughs,
his mother has lost him.

PANSELINOS

We stumble down the mountain, whipped
with sun, drowned by the blue
giant heaving below us.
We whisper to each other once, again,
like an incantation,
        Almond blossoms smell like honey.

It's spring, it's coming tonight,
the full moon of April, newborn lamb
still round and sleek in the sky.

Late dusk, we're hungry, we haven't eaten
since dawn, we watch the backbone of the cliff
arch over night's arms, we see night's mouth
devour the day. You turn, look at me
and say, I'm starving.

We walk to the village square
where children dance in awe under the lamps,
watching the halo of moths grow and burn.
Each of us a witness to light
bred by darkness.

We live under the sun, but it's the moon we worship, *la luna*,
the moon, *to fengari*, the mysterious lover,
she's coming out tonight, complete, *panselinos*,
completely naked, while we sit here swallowing oysters,
watching her shoulders shimmer below the hills.

Impossible opal, glowing round bone.
I cannot believe there are footprints on her body.
I do not believe that men know what she's made of.

We're waiting for her, you and I,
drawing the violin bow of this wine
over and down our tongues.

Her back clears the mountains now, slowly,
she floats like a jewel high above our hands.
We cannot name the orchard of stars
but we know the moon, *panselinos,* April, she floods
the sky with an original sea, spills silver
in the Aegean, heaves a tide of unearthly blue
above us, a shade my words fail to conjure,
        the indigo heart of a seahorse,
        Athena's irises after love.

The moon is a pearl made for the palm of a goddess,
la luna is a pool of milk.
Somewhere in the village, a woman wakes
to nurse her youngest son.
She stands at the open window,
hair glowing with the dark.
She smiles when the child reaches
open-mouthed to the window, thirsty,
his small hands stretching for the moon.

On this island of sheep and spiders, lost hedgehogs,
I discover a starving dog and her three naked saviours,
giggling savages in the sun.
    We're learning Greek. We live here now, they say,
      tossing me their snorkel.

The oldest boy is Adam.
His body was blessed at birth by a dolphin.
He shows me how to follow the green fish with purple fins.
We play tag in underwater Byzantium,
push and drift through palaces of rays and urchins and eels.
In slow-motion blue, he waltzes me around pillars
      of sunlight, proving the sea
      and nothing else holds up the horizon.
Adam does not fall but dives down grinning,
      returns with a handful of sand
      to show he's touched the rippled belly of the Aegean.

Later, on the beach, the youngest boy reveals
a perfect red pebble in his wet palm.
This is a ruby-growing stone, he declares.
Ah, six-year-old wisdom, my master of tornadoes
and Oz, owner of Dorothy's red shoes:
    How can I doubt you?

The land of passionate deities imparts a simple prayer:
Please give me this.

These trees and flowers, a thousand monstrous beauties
      of red wasp and black beetle,
      each bat diving under a lake of stars,
      all the living stones:
      charms in this garden.
Every road of rock and dust a path through this garden.

While the moon's silver tongue licks salt from the sea,
    the children show me rose quartz and old coins,
        jelly-fish and dinosaur eggs.
Under that field of mint, they explain, *is an ancient cemetery.*
Dead B.C. people live there, affirms the boy
    with the magic shoes.

Eyes wide, he whispers, *That's how we got here.*
    I just said There's no place like home
        There's no place like home,
        then tapped my red heels together.
        When we opened our eyes, we were here!

When I laugh, he becomes angry.
Really, he insists, *it's true.*

Suddenly I see he's not joking.
It is true, for those welcomed by these shores.
When we open our eyes, we are right *here*,
eating cucumbers and feta on Sappho's sand,
sienna-naked, in mad love with the day.

ANTIGONE

Antigone at dusk,
her back to Sympathy.
A woman in a white shirt
sitting in the sand.
It is impossible for you
to know her now, though you
recall the legend of her name.

Darkness slowly fills the air
with purple sand.
Departure.
Her eyes launch into the Aegean.
Her hair is like a black mare's mane.
The entire sea gradually becomes
the colour of this hair.

Antigone.
You call out to her, perhaps,
but she does not recognize your voice.
She does not recognize the beauty
of her own face.

Antigone is gone,
though her shirt still glows
white like a sail.
She might be arriving now
in a new country.
She sits in the sand,
salt dried on her hands
like bone-dust.

You can hear the voices
of small children
playing around her
like lunar moths
around a cold star.

LATE AUGUST ON LESVOS

Late August on Lesvos, the garden thickens with seed.
A Babylon of butterflies seduces the flowers.
Dawn and dusk, nectar rises in saffron tides.
Even the sea shines like a giant's bowl of honey.

Yiorgos and I live in a chaos of watermelons.
Mikhaili heaves the green treasures to his pigs.
Panagos rolls them under every bench
and bed in the house.
Goats trip over them and donkeys sink
grateful teeth into the cool rinds.

Black seeds root in our bellies, send tendrils
of jewel up our spines.
Our dreams are vines winding us
into the astonishing red halls of dawn.

August, yes, I sleep outside and wake at five
to fourteen goddesses setting the stage of the world.
They paint the backdrop of this extravagant theatre
shades of ruby and violet, a flawless set, silhouette
of stone house and fence and grape vine
sprawling black against the sky.

Beyond the road, fig trees stretch awkward white arms
above mauve thistles, yellow thorns.
A thousand years later, the desert souls
are still humbled by their fruit:
        green sea anemones hide crimson tentacles of sugar.

August on the island, before I open my eyes
I hear the kittens purring, feel the white dog curled
in the crook of my knees, her fur a miracle of new snow.
Sometimes the black goat escapes and wakes me herself,
two cleft hooves knocking on my chest,
velvet nose at my ear.

Feast of late summer, the sun exhausts the gardens,
the valley is an upturned table, spilling,
spilling, tomatoes like edible rubies,
almonds splashing into the water basin,
stars falling from the sky like fruit.

Deep August on the island, the dazzling blade of days
pares the moon down until it hangs beyond us
like one bloodied fang of the tigress.

Always the light speaks first,
light, who writes her own chant in passing,
the way brilliance deepens as it fades.

The first day of September is still summer,
old women say, but the heat stands up
like a lover denied and walks away
so slowly, glancing back,
back down the path, pulling fistfuls
of leaves from the trees.

The gardens fill with amber-red sugar,
 tangles of goat-skin in the dust,
 baskets barren but dripping dusk.

Still summer, the old shepherd says,
waving wrinkled hands through kindled air,
but what do we see in the skeleton-vines
and the footprints haunted by ants?

What do we finally harvest from gardens
but the gold weight of death,
that heavy fruit,
its frightening grace.

Among mouse droppings, dust in the urgent papers,
I find your last letter, tales of children and garlic
and spring gliding into your valley
like a woman flying down a slide.

I don't know if you've written since then.
Chaos is a Greek word:
    Athenian politics have poisoned the mailman,
    strikes all summer long, no signs
    from my cold-rock country.
The cities sink into memory's sediment, wide streets awash
with red and yellow leaves, first ice-water
wind of autumn splashing the neck.
The people there grow a fleece of dust.

Your last letter.
Grit envelopes the paper now, sepia
seeps in from the sun-curled edges.
I've circled the date, *May 7, late evening*

but this morning, September swallows her tail
like a famished snake, the hot scales
of summer disappear and a chill wind
rides in, prophecying winter.
The ants' desperation is contagious.
They rush in a hunt for the edible,
tracking earth, ankles, walls, drowning
in the marmalade and milk pails, licking
the essence out of walnut shells.
How do those tiny slaves
own such mammoth hunger?

Have the ants in your garden already gone underground?
It's colder there, frost and gloves in the morning.
Let me remember where you live.
Where you live
hold that phrase in the mouth,
taste its small but supreme weight,
a bloodstone on the tongue.

I know you wake up early.
Jam sweetens your fingers, children's voices
rise, plunge like swallows, so quickly,
perpetual bearers of sunlight.

Where are the windows
in that house I've never seen?
I didn't live in houses this year.
I existed on trains.
Even the rooms I slept in
were abandoned compartments
whose close walls whispered,
Do not rest here, do not stay.

Cities close to borders claimed my life
until I came to the island,
took the sea as my frontier and washed
Baudelaire's acidic verses from my eyes.
Finally this exile teaches me
to seek the greeting, not the escape,
of the roads beneath my feet.

I've dreamt my body as a storm,
but this season the calm rolls closer,
from the east.

Have I found a place to rest?
Across the water, the hills of Turkey
shimmer and sway like a purple caravan.

You can't quite see it, can you?
No, nor these hills carved from the gold
and olive-green thigh bones of God.
My words will never hold
the wind and light of these hours.
I don't know what to do
with the grace here, where to offer
my prayers when the temples stand in ruins.

I want to give you this place
like the exotic fruit we were denied
as children, press it deeply
into your palm and whisper,
            Taste this, Eve's sin,
            eat the same ripe glory.

I'm returning soon, to stay
until your children know my voice again.
Figs dried under this sun are yours,
a sac of almonds, this cologne
of goats and ouzo.

I will smash a glass, offer you a Turkish cigarette.
We'll lean together while the windows
deepen like cold wells, reflect faces
drowning in the swell of night and time.

But even this will not still our hands,
our voices praising
the miracles of our age.

VOULA

*Rebetiko is a hypnotic, passionate style of music which
became popular in Greece in the 1930's and '40's. It was, and
still is, the music of the poor and of social outcasts, similar in
many ways to Gypsy Flamenco. Traditionally it is played and
danced only by men.*

Little spot

is the meaning of my name,
but look at me, my life
is big as the sun, I am Voula,
I am famous.

She is ugly, they'll tell you,
a dirty-dog woman, a junkie
covered in sores
and a bitch besides,

but look at my young lovers,
tekna-mou,
Sonia from Brazil,
Katerina from the north,
Sinead from Ireland with
all her silk and lace.

I am Voula
I am famous.

If you see me dance to *rebetiko*
you too will love me,
you will watch and look away
with burning eyes.
Even Vaso's plates know
the disorder of love, they leap
off the tables and shatter
just to touch my feet.

With these scuffed boots
I sway hard and slow inside
the music, my arms in the air,
elbows crooked above my head:
I am balancing each star
high above the plane trees.

I close my eyes to dance like this.
You have to close your eyes
to see inside music,
to see inside a woman,
and to see inside the gods.

The accordion and I
breathe the warm night wind.
The mandolin has my curves,
the same thin hardness and dirty
fingerprints all over her body.

Sweat shines like oil on my forehead.
I dance so slowly, a snake
without legs, without arms,
held up by the taut nerves
of music.

I have given my limbs to you.
I have given my eyes to you.
I am naked in my dance,
in this night
under the plane trees.

Na zeseis hilia kronia!
Na zeseis panda!

May you live a thousand years.
May you live forever.